mo+th

Issue Number One
+ SUMMER 2005

Los Angeles Poets & Writers Collective

Bombshelter Press
+ LOS ANGELES

mo+th

Issue Number One

Summer 2005

EDITOR: Vicki Whicker

SERIES EDITOR: Jack Grapes

LAYOUT & DESIGN: Alan Berman

COVER DESIGN & DIGITAL ART: Ellen Jantzen

mo+th is published by Bombshelter Press. Contributing authors are members of the Los Angeles Poets & Writers Collective, which sponsors writing workshops, readings, seminars, retreats, and literary publications including *ONTHEBUS*, *Wednesday*, and mo+th. We do not accept unsolicited submissions. Subscriptions and general correspondence should be sent to Bombshelter Press, P.O. Box 481266, Bicentennial Station, Los Angeles CA 90048. Single copies of mo+th can be ordered for $12.50 plus $1.50 shipping. A subscription for 4 issues costs $45 (postpaid).

info@bombshelterpress.com

www.bombshelterpress.com

Los Angeles Poets & Writers Collective

www.jackgrapes.com

back cover:

"If one knows exactly what one is going to do, what's the point of doing it."
—*Pablo Picasso*

"Writing is an act of love. If it's not, it's only scribbling."
—*Jean Cocteau*

SHARON BARR
Hear Quake 7

LESLIE BERLIANT
The Beating of Moth Wings 9

A. ALEXANDER BLOOM
I Wish I Could Have Met Her 11

ESTHER BRADLEY–DETALLY
Children of the Stolen Ones 12

REBECCA CLITES
Discovery 13

JD CULLUM
The One That Got Away 14

FRANCINE DEVETTE
Do I, Will I, Have the Stuff? 15

STEPHANIE DIANI
Grey 16

LORA McPHAIL &
MICHAEL JANTZEN (L&M)
Interview with Ellen Jantzen 18

TIM GIBLIN
Flagstone 21

MANNY GLASER
My Mother Wouldn't Nurse Me 23

ALICE HAYWARD
Island Togetherness 25

ABIGAIL JONES
Gothic Parking 27

ERICA JORDAN
Alzheimer's & Old Lace 28

iii

JEAN KATZ
    Regret 30

JUDI KAUFMAN
    I Am an Island 31
    Legs Spread Wide 31

RONI KELLER
    Thrive Again 32

FLO LAWRENCE
    Gone Lost 33

ANTHONY A. LEE
    Father 35

ROZ LEVINE
    A Site for the Sacred 37

KAREN MACEDONIO
    Gathering the Pieces 38

JEAN MANDEL
    This Wasn't Christmas or Thanksgiving 39

KÄTHE MAZUR
    Sharing 40

MARIANA MEDOFF
    She Prepares His Coffee 42

ELAINE MINTZER
    from Till 43

VICKI WHICKER (VW)
    Interview with Elaine Mintzer 45

BILL MOSELEY
    Green Belt 48

SHANNON MURPHY
    gluttonous sunburned men 49

ANGELLA NAZARIAN
    It's Always the Mother 51

VANESSA POSTER
    His Loss 53

GIL PULDE
    Talking to Stars 54

HILLARY RUBIN
    Blue Skies 55

BONNIE SCHROEDER
    What's in a Name? 57

DIANE SHERLOCK
    MadWomenRun 58

JUNE SHIGENO
    Rainy Days Cover-Up 60

HANNAH SILBERMAN
    Pendulum 61

AMY SLOMOVITS
    Milk and Music 63

MEWS SMALL
    Sirens 64

BRITTANY MICHELLE SMITH-WATTS
    Your love 65

JACK SUNDMACHER
    Root Canal 66

CAROL ANN SUSI
    The Brooklyn Woman of the World 68

MARK VALLEY
    Scorpio Moon 70

WHITNEY WALKER
    Imago 71

CYNTHIA WANDS
    A Lesson in Feeding Ducks 72

MAY'AAN LESLIE WEISS
    Maiden Voyage 74

KEDREN WERNER
    Tea and Sympathy 77

VICKI WHICKER
    Abbot Kinney's Dirty Dream 79

KATHLEEN ZEISLER GOLDMAN
    Some Other Alice, Some Other Land 81

It was a slow Saturday. We folded errands in amidst exercise. We went to the regular stores. We went to the regular stores and performed the regular activities with the regular resistance. I wondered, as I regularly did, if I would feel more fulfilled if I lived in Europe . . . Paris specifically. London would be nice, but so expensive. Italy would be a whole other choice . . . more advanced. That would take even more courage, as I don't speak Italian. I love going there but organizing a whole life that would be hard. Or maybe not.

Paris . . . that was my city. I would sharpen my French . . . an immersion course immediately. I would inhale its magnificence, learn to cook, really cook. I would learn about sauces . . . become a 'saucier.' He would love it too. I know it. It would add another dimension to our relationship . . . to our lives! Did we need another dimension? Did we need? Neediness . . . that was not us. We were happy. But routine had set in. Routine had been allowed to enter and set up residence. It permeated our lives like an oil spill. That we were getting older was undeniable. So it was time to break out and do things differently. Time to change everything or calcify!

That Saturday we had the usual discord over restaurant choices. We ended up at the most convenient place, the restaurant where we were the most comfortable, the most at ease.

It had become a life of ease. Maybe that's why I wanted to change everything.

We had a nice dinner. I had lamb chops and champagne. He had the seafood pasta special. We loved each other.

It took forever to get our car. There was a new valet. We got home. I let our dog out. My husband lay down. His acid reflux was bugging him again. I told him to walk around, that lying down was the worst thing . . . another conversation re-run. He said he was too tired to move. I washed my face, brought the dog in, turned out the lights and locked the doors. I wandered around chattering about little things that had happened that day.

As I came in the bedroom I noticed he looked frightened. His color was different. "I can't breathe" he gasped. I felt a black horror take hold of me. This was different. This was new. Moochi barked at the back door wanting to get back out. A car radio blasted from the street.

He was in pain.

He needed something.

He was draining out.

I went for the phone.

He grabbed my hand. "It hurts. I don't know what's wrong."

"Don't worry honey, I'm getting help."

911 . . . seconds seemed hours.

They would send help.

"Start compressions," they said.

I'd only done this on a dummy . . . never with my own heart.

"Oh God oh God oh God . . . let him be ok. I'll do anything. I'll be anybody you want me to be. Just let him be OK."

He reached up and grabbed me.

He gasped for air.

"Don't let go . . . I need you!" I screamed.

"YOU ARE MY LIFE!"

He released and relaxed.

"He's OK he's gonna be OK," I thought.

He gripped me again and gasped again.

And then relaxed.

The paramedics rushed in, dragging a crash cart.

They went to work . . . methodically, rhythmically.

I held his head . . . it felt cold or maybe it was just me.

I left my body and hovered above watching all the activity, not sure what to feel.

If I went back there it would hurt so bad. It would hurt like nothing had ever hurt before.

There would be no one to hold onto because the person that I always held onto was gone. He would never come through the door again; never give me his coat when I was cold; never argue over a restaurant choice or the color to paint the living room. We would never move to Paris or fly in a jet together holding hands on take off or in a restaurant or the car. We would never kiss and make up or wake up together . . . or grow old together. "How can I go back there? I want to stay with you . . . please don't leave me. God save me. Take me not him. I can leave but I can't stay!"

"Can we call somebody for you?" I heard a voice say.

And then the horrible hurt rushed in, as if it too would become part of the routine.

She makes her way through the farmers market that smells of over ripe melons and horse manure out of routine, she doesn't really need anything. One handle of her blue straw bag is frayed, only a few remaining strands hold it together, stronger than they appear. The defect does not deter her from loading the bag each week with jars of honey, carafes of olive oil, heavy cantaloupes and pounds of stone fruit.

She struggles to finish it all before it molds from the damp sea air, trying to assess which melon is the softest every morning and whether this peach or that plum can last another day. The decay starts with a few brown spots and ends up rotting the fruit black from the inside out. Her freezer holds 22 pounds of apricots that cost $32 for the privilege of carrying home a box of golden, round fruit that smelled of summer. She will bake a few pounds each month to recapture the hum of bees and the scent of grass when her apartment does not already carry the heady sweet smell of ripened fruit, even with the windows wide open to the cool gray, morning fog.

The fog reminds her of childhood vacations, waking her father at dawn to search the beach for a perfect Sand Dollar or elusive conch shell. Pulling at the tops peaking out, the only remains of shells long ago eroded. Just once, the soaked sand created a vacuum that resisted her tugs and as the watery suction released, she extracted a perfectly in tact giant conch. After that, even a pristine white sand dollar could not compare to the excitement of the conch shell. Her father did not comment if he event noticed that she stopped coming to his bedside each morning, her blue and white checked sun hat tied tight under her chin, ready for the first rays of light on the beach.

She is not wasteful, but the colors, smells, and textures of markets put her into a trance until on her walk home the spell breaks and she realizes she has too much. A few weeks ago she had to throw out all the baking supplies from her pantry. Bags of wheat, rye and barley flour, blocks of exotic chocolate, rice paper and lavender honey all infested with worms and moths from too many years of sitting idle, waiting to be used. For months, she pretended that she could control the moths, squeezing them in little bits of paper towel when they would appear. But one night she felt the wind rush of hundreds of wings flapping as she lay in her bed and she knew that it was time. She stayed up all night watching the worms burrowing in the chocolate and the cocoons swaying on the rice paper. In the morning, she swept all of the ingredients into the garbage.

At the artichoke stand, she runs her fingers over the pointy tips, and feels a tap on her shoulder. She steps to the side without looking until a familiar voice says "hey." She twists to look at him, the skin of her left index finger still impaled on the top of an artichoke. It is Josiah and he is smiling. She knows that he will be proud of himself for finding her here. He likes it when he can demonstrate that he knows her habits. She is not sure why it matters to him, after all, awareness of patterns is no replacement for intimacy.

She disengages her finger from the spike and turns to face him. "I've been trying to call you," he reprimands, "where have you been?" She turns her palms up and shrugs. He notices the drop of blood on her finger tip. "Let's go sit in the grass," he says. They find a small open patch of grass in the shade, surrounded by people. Young couples in tank tops and shorts, feed each other bites of omelets and crepes. Kids with tattooed arms and ankles, sit in circles, toe rings and metal bracelets glinting in the sun. Families park strollers next to plaid blankets, dad stretched out looking on satisfied as mom takes the little one for a pony ride. She finds it hard to breathe, enveloped by so much living.

"I am moving," he tells her. "That is why I have been trying to reach you." "Where are you moving to?" she asks, already knowing the answer. "New York, to be with Marissa," he says. "When are you leaving?" she asks. What is this she's feeling, she wonders. Sadness, jealousy, anger? "At the end of this month," he says. "I have been trying to call you," he says again. She can feel the image creeping up on her, appearing as it does anytime she might feel an inkling of normal, every day disappointment. Cold, gray winter. Dirty snow on the ground. People crying, all those hands reaching out to touch her, hug her. A chorus of "I'm so sorry" "such a tragedy" and "if there is anything you need" is ringing in her ears. Two caskets. One large, one small. Two caskets and dirty snow. Black gloves on her hands, the hands everyone wants to hold, the hands of a mourner, the hands of a widow, the hands of a dead child's mother. And then the image is gone. It has done its job, erased any emotion, any reaction she might have to today, to this moment. There is only one moment to be experienced for the rest of her life.

She was a beauty with dyed black hair and green eyes. During her last days here she caused ruckus in the bars. Dry Rob Roy was her drink. She pounded them fast. Her mouth was big. The bartender called the cops. Often, they took her to a mental hospital for observation. "She put on such a great show. She really pulled the wool over every one's eyes when it came time to, when she needed to," he said to me as I sat down by his hospital bed. He, Donald Mesiti, was her last husband, number five. The Italian one I had heard stories about from my mother, his stepdaughter, forty years ago. The staunch Union worker! The socialist! The one who worked the printing press at the Herald Tribune! The one who wrote plays in his free time! The one who used to come home covered in ink stains! The one she beat with a frying pan in a drunken rage! The only husband who ever left her! Yes, that one. I finally got to meet him. I got to meet him right before he died of throat cancer, thirty years after she died of breast cancer. He chuckled, "One time we were at Bellevue. We were sitting on a bench waiting. A female psychiatrist came down the staircase. She overwhelmed the psychiatrist. She out smarted her, she was a brilliant talker," he said. "She had convinced the psychiatrist that nothing was wrong with her. She was proficient. She became a new person. But I knew some thing was wrong with her. They could never hold her. We walked out the corridor on to the street and into the first bar we found."

I wish I could have saved "her," "she," my grandmother, Joyce Frances Denny.

for Gloria Haithman

"Greens" makes me think of Ola Mae's Greens, down in my belly in Olean, the western part of New York, where crowds of us burst into Ola Mae's Restaurant to shoot the breeze, and eat her famous Greens.

Here in Pasadena, California, the subject of greens and chitlins came up. I thought of Ola Mae's place: the camaraderie, her corn bread too, her open heart, and her Best Greens-Cook-in-the-World Self. Wednesday night Gloria talked about the same thing, but also spoke of soul food of another kind: of love and hope and faith. Gloria said, "We were not born colored! We came in that way. "Yeah baby," I thought, "No Crayola used in this process," and then a phrase entered the room, as Gloria told about the African-American Baha'i Sisters on a tour of South Africa.

These Sisters, they met some African women who stared at them, looked long and hard, as Gloria and Aurore saw the "Who Are They" question form in the women's brown eyes."Why," said one of the African women, "These visitors are The Children of the Stolen Ones."

Measure this phrase out on the tongue, slowly, "The Stol . . . The Stolen . . . The Stolen Ones." "Children of the Stolen Ones." Feel your heart melt as a great and timeless grief is finally acknowledged.

I'm no artist, and I live in a world that thinks it knows its colors; knows colors inside lines, not outside; "lines" being the operative word. Name every quality our sisters, our brothers, of African Heritage carry with fortitude, and you come up with, in my book. "The Chosen Ones." Hmmm. "Chosen." "Stolen."

What if God saw that these Chosen Ones endured trials similar to the Minor Prophets?

And what if the Ancient Beauty knew His love for His Chosen Ones, knew they suffered: the banishment, the chains, the whippings, as His Prophets and Messengers in the Path of God?

What if this planet is a testing ground to see who can show courage under fire. But wait, here's another view: the Children of the Stolen Ones, their children, their children's children, are the Morning Glories for our time. It's the story Morning Glory! Let's proclaim, let's shout, herald our ransomed ancestors, that we might re-frame our hearts. Let's join each other in history's future where lines are a thing of the past and colors are loved-filled stripes of every hue.

I pray to fools.
My church is a circus run by no man.
This religion has no boundaries.
Every graceful risk has been taken from me.
And my soul is deemed a farce.
I remember all who attempt to persuade me.
Never will I succumb to the wants of others.
Lines are for those who can wait—
Patience is a sin when time is running out.
Lesser creatures run to find me—
The prize will disappoint.
And the clowns will cry on my feet.
Amen.

13

In the box on my computer screen, I see a metal chair and part of a table. The door squeaks open, voices are heard, and a man is lead into the room by a larger man who is only seen from the back. I can tell the larger man is a detective because I see the outline of his bulletproof vest. The suspect's hair is black, balding slightly on top. He has a wide black mustache. His face is unshaven. The officer punches in a few numbers on a cell phone, then places his keys on the table. The officer leaves the room.

The man sniffs and wipes his nose. He crosses and uncrosses his legs, which are jiggling. He pants are baggy. He appears to be wearing socks or perhaps shoes the same color as his pants which are pale khaki. His rumpled t-shirt has a whimsical pattern: blue fireworks. He wipes his brow, picks at his eyes and eyebrows.

The officer comes back with a cup of coffee for himself and a bottle of water for the man. "Tenk you," the man murmurs as the officer holds out a bottle, saying, "Here you go, Senior." The officer steps out of the room again. The man is alone. The video clip is going to be over soon because the bar at the bottom of the box is halfway complete. My face is not moving at all. My mouth is open and I can hear myself breathing through my nose. I sound like a large sleeping dog.

The man reaches into his pocket and places something on the table. It appears to be a coin. Then, he reaches for the water bottle, cracks the cap off. He takes one sip, swallows. I can hear the water whistling from the bottle. Then, as if an afterthought, he takes another sip. His movements quicken now. He caps the bottle, places it back on the table. He tugs at his shirt, and pulls from his pants a gun. I briefly see his white belly. He inhales as he snaps the safety off and positions the gun at his temple.

The street outside is as quiet as a field. My office seems like an accident of papers and equipment, as if everything landed from the sky. Tonight I have seen a man who fed strips of his face to his dog, the pussy outcome of a brown spider bite, a head on a fence post, another man impaled on telephone pole. I've worked my way down to the bottom, to the last link: A Suspect Commits Suicide in Interrogation Room. I am wearing a bathrobe and slippers. I have been eating pretzels. Dough is impacted into my molars and my lips are salty.

The marine layer drifts through the screen. The man's belly was white and hairless, like a boy's. Forty-seven years old. Fresh from a San Bernardino car chase. Fresh from shooting a police officer. His gun is long and superior, the finest thing in the room.

He shoots into his head. His head and arm jerk apart from each other. The "Auhh." he makes sounds like an orgasm. The legs thrust out like an impatient toddler. The left eye darkens and wells up with blood. The room is vacant now. I should go to bed.

A noise of scraping feet and then the officer says, "Ah, fuck!" off camera.

"What happened?" another voice asks. The officer enters frame with another man behind him. The backs of two heads, alive heads, brains in warm Western blood.

"Nobody shook him." The officer gathers his keys and his cup of coffee from off the table. "Fuck." he says.

The body is alone. Gun in the left hand, resting on the lap. Water bottle and coin on the table. The tape rolls on. I am disappointed. The right hand slides from its place and drops toward the floor. Blood falls from the chair. The clip stops.

Francine DeVette + *Do I, Will I, Have the Stuff?*

Today I am empty. Empty voice, empty mind. Oh yeah . . . this is familiar . . . going all the way back to guess where? . . . Kindergarten.

It was a very special day for the parents of this classroom full of four-year-olds, especially this four-year-old. The excitement and bustle was tinging my skin. I don't think I was truly aware of the purpose of the day or my role. I just kind of liked it. I liked all the people and I liked the school. And I had extreme four-year-old confidence. You know, the confidence that comes from pure joy, a joy that knows no previous loss. It's uncontainable. It bursts from a child's body. No wonder I could hardly sit or stand still. But the time to be still had finally come. Mrs. Herman, our teacher who was probably 50 but looked 80 to me, stood in front of the classroom in her dark plaid dress and old lady shoes and called out my name.

"Francine!" She was pointing to the mock-clock whose big hand she put on the twelve and the little hand on the eight. "What time is it?"

Whoa, wait a minute. Am I in a situation where I'm supposed to know something and then be able to tell it? I choked! All I see are children's eyes looking at me and waiting. We all had been placed in tiny chairs, around tiny round tables, all over the room. The Mommies were seated like soldiers in chairs along all the walls. The steamy radiators below the big closed windows were keeping the room cozy warm in the middle of this wintry day. I see my Mom's eyes, she is also looking and waiting. She looks pristine and perfectly dressed. Her scarf, tied around her angora sweater, brought out the green in her skirt and I see bare stocking legs peeking out from her wool skirt.

I did not like this brand-new, icky, feeling of panic coming on . . . I did not like it! Right now the brightness of the sun was shining and displaying our previously drawn crayoned pictures as well as our little drums and instruments that had been placed in boxes in the corner, and the special hook section with our names written above to hang our coats and hats. Normally, I loved this room. But this warm sun was now exposing me and the blankness of my face.

My mind, my thoughts or wherever you go, to figure out how to get the answer to the teacher's question was gone.

I was empty and in the empty was everybody's eyes . . . waiting. I thought if this is what life is, if this is what is expected of me, if we need to be answering things on cue, (of course I didn't know the word cue then) then I guess I didn't have the stuff. By now, I was paralyzed, fully, like deer in the headlight kind of thing. The room blurred. I think my fear of being blank was causing the fight or flight mechanism to kick in and blurring was a four-year-old's best attempt at the flight part. I wish I had known how to faint.

"Francine! Francine!" The teacher's voice broke the air, "What time is it?" I looked up, opened my mouth and the words eight o'clock magically came out. The tension in the room broke. The teacher, the Moms, my Mommy and all the children were happy and relieved and off went Mrs. Herman to question the next child.

I suppose I should also be happy as I look back at that moment when the answer had finally come to me and bask in that success. Unfortunately, though, what really stuck forever was the coming up empty.

"Ok, I'm going to take this big lens and this big light and we're going to put white vinegar on your cervix . . ." he said. Big lens, big light—was I, a four-year-old? "And if it turns white, then I may do a pinch biopsy." A what?

I'm already splayed out like a chicken to be dressed on the grey Naugahyde chair, feet in metal stirrups made less cold by grey cotton covers labeled "FAITH" all in caps; my ass, under the green-grey plastic sheet, is sticking to white butcher paper. My arms hold the green paper close to my sides. I'm definitely a chicken waiting to be slaughtered. And this guy, this doctor, is going to probe my insides, maybe pull out a piece, make room for stuffing his instruments or his medicines up inside to make me taste better. Chicken. It's what's for dinner.

"Why do the stirrups say 'faith'?" I ask.

He looks puzzled, almost alarmed, then understands. "Oh, it's a pharmaceutical product. It's an acronym." He doesn't say what the letters stand for and I supply "Furry Ass In The Hole" in my head. He makes me lie back and flips on his 'bright light' and aims his 'big lens' at me.

His face is hidden now behind a mechanical eye; the lens focused on my vagina and cervix. I see a bright light and a doctor's white-coated torso. Behind him is the impersonal face of a female nurse. Her face is blank, but I insert on it skepticism, boredom, criticism at the size/shape/color of my insides. The pink doesn't match the decor. Everything else in the room is grey—ceiling, floors, walls, cabinets. It smells grey; the words spoken sound grey. The speculum is cold grey and the vinegar he repeatedly swabs inside feels grey. Like death.

It also feels like he's been looking for a long while. It feels like he can see everything—the cat fur underneath our bed where I never vacuum, the kitchen floor, unmopped these past few months, the stacks of paperwork—financial and medical—that I haven't yet dealt with. He can definitely see that the cosmetician who performed my last bikini was incredibly thorough. He can see my self-doubt, my anxiety, the shiny grey coat of guilt wrapped around my heart and lungs. He just spotted the time that I peed my pants at age five for no good reason, standing alone on the cracked and burning sidewalk one summer morning in front of my parent's tract house. I stood there, paralyzed then too, with warm water running down one leg to puddle on the cement and watched cars go by, certain that they saw me and what I was doing and were also ashamed. Paralyzed. He knew more about me now than I did. I was a butterfly, pinned to his exam room chair, waiting to be set free or snuffed out after being studied, gradually turning grey in captivity.

"Well," he paused for a full minute. Oh shit, long pauses were bad. "It all looks normal to me. There was one patch . . ." My butterfly colors came back as he rattled on, "but I think that's normal" More phrases . . . "every four months until it's normal" . . . "good to get it checked" . . . "stress" . . . and then, "Ok, you can get up, you're done."

The grey was gone, he removed the pin, I was free!

After he left the room, I folded up the plastic green anxiety blanket that had covered my lap and placed it on the butcher paper. I breathed, inhaled back into myself my childhood dramas, my dirty floors and my skeptical nurses. My grey, cancerous chrysalis lay on the paper next to the blanket. And I left it there when I walked out of the room, having been declared whole by a stranger in a white coat.

17

Lora McPhail &
Michael Jantzen (L&M) **+ *Interview with Ellen Jantzen***

*This issue's cover features Ellen Jantzen's **moth image 5**, a piece in the Artificial Evolution series of electronic art that she has produced. Ellen is an electronic artist as well as a longstanding member of the Los Angeles Poets and Writers Collective. Her interview with Lora McPhail and Michael Jantzen, first published online at www.netartreview.com and excerpted here, gives insight into Ellen's artistic process. Ellen's most recent works can be seen at www.etavonni.com.*

L&M: Briefly introduce us to the key formal and thematic issues in this current body of images.

Ellen: My most current body of images, a series titled Artificial Evolution, thematically deals with creating hybrid life forms; life forms that may include manmade elements in the mix. The key formal element is symmetry. I have use symmetry in earlier works to some degree but feel my use here directly reflects the symmetry seen in most life forms.

L&M: What do you think are some of the most important things in life that inspire you to do the work that you do? How do you develop your hybridizations and/or elemental relationships?

Ellen: First of all, I create to give meaning to my life. I draw inspiration from the natural world; rock formations, seed pods, nests; shapes that resonate with reproduction, growth and repetition. I feel compelled to work in ways that create meaning. I pull from somewhere deep inside, not from a purely analytical space, so my hybridizations are very spontaneous and uncalculated. They are developed subconsciously then meaning is assigned as I refine and title each piece.

L&M: Can you describe how the relationship between the original photo-shoot setups and the final digitally enhanced images has evolved in your work, as you have become more invested in the medium?

Ellen: I do a lot of playing around, testing different relationships and locations. I take dozens and dozens of photographs of my setups and may end up only producing a few final pieces from that abundance. As I become more invested in the medium, I have

18

come to better understand what the out comes of my setups will be. For instance, I have become fascinated with translucency and find that more and more I include some translucent element in my setups. This allows me to control and direct light in interesting ways. While I am becoming more "skilled" at understanding the relationships and possibilities of each setup as it pertains to my image making process, I sometimes purposefully create random setups for their unforeseen potential.

L&M: Referring to your own experience as a designer, what aspects of the media best serve your vision and/or process? Is there something uniquely inherent about the computer (and how you use it to create your work) that urges innovation, if so, what do you think this is?

Ellen: As a designer, I have been drawn to working in a hands-on manner with three-dimensional forms. All along I have also been drawn to two-dimensional work, especially graphics. With the advent of the personal computer and ever-increasingly sophisticated computer graphics software, I have been able to combine my desires into one direction. The computer allows me to see in new ways; it allow me to be surprised by the outcome and the possibilities. The computer urges innovation by presenting almost limitless options; it is up to me to say "stop" when I deem something new and different is worthy of saving. Again, because I have so many source photos to draw from, I save, initially, hundreds of images. From these, the selection, the editing, begins.

L&M: What kind of equipment and or technologies do you wish you had access to that you don't, and how might these things help to advance the integrity of your work?

Ellen: Well, I could always use a more powerful computer with a larger screen, a higher megapixel camera, a bigger format printer . . . on and on, but these wouldn't really advance the integrity of my work, just make what I currently do quicker. What I would like to investigate next is animation. Of course I'd need software and time to learn. I feel that I could successfully create short animations of my hybrids where they would take form right before your eyes.

L&M: Have you thought of experimenting with similar themes and aesthetics in other media? How do you feel scale, dimension and time influence your work?

Ellen: Yes, animation would be a new direction I would like to experiment with. I also would like to experiment with creating three-dimensional sculptures based on some of my hybrid images. I think this would be rather interesting; to go from a three-dimensional setup to a two-dimensional image and back to a new three-dimensional hybrid object where I would have had to interpret the full three-dimensionality of the flat image.

The scale of my work, currently, is quite intimate. Both my images and setups are under three feet or so and the dimensions accommodate the photo format to some degree. I can foresee creating some grand scale setups using large landforms as more that backdrops. Perhaps my hybrids would become human scale. I would then want my images to be quite large also, mural-scale perhaps, to emphasize the human scale aspect allowing viewers to interact with the images.

Time influences my work in several ways, time of day and time of year (seasonal changes and light angles). I also like to use the time advancement of a given situation. For instance, a series of photo setups I took right after a thunderstorm that goes from a very gray sky and muted look to a rainbow to sun rimmed clouds with sunbeams illuminating the setup. Also, conceptually, I am speeding up time by "evolving" my hybrids in a matter of hours.

L&M: How conscious are you while you are working, that what you finally present as your art may have any political relevance? And, if your work is perceived by some to be politically relevant, how important is this to you?

Ellen: I have varied political concerns from poverty and hunger to issues of war. These are in the background as I create, influencing but not directly guiding my directions. I am concerned with GMOs (genetically modified organisms) and how corporations are controlling more and more of plant and animal life. I am concerned with indigenous people being bullied into purchasing their seed rather than saving seed from the year before. But, I feel there are activists much more gifted politically than I am who can address these, and so many other issues, straight on intellectually. I want to deal with the emotional side of charged issues through my art by addressing them in an allusive manner. I also have written poetry, trying to put feelings into words but found that my medium is mainly the visual.

L&M: How might you see your work developing to address these concerns ever more directly? How do you hope other people will most be influenced by you, and your work?

Ellen: I don't want to develop a more direct approach, at least not in the near future. Again, I feel what I have to offer is a unique vision that includes my concern with living entities and the natural world without being preachy or specific. I hope my work inspires others to create in their own way; to address their issues of concern in personal terms that are unique to them.

I was hanging out with Chris from NY earlier today, having breakfast at Mel's Diner, talking about September 11th and car crashes. I've had a bubble around me, protecting me my whole life. Its funny like that, two guys getting together from NY and the conversation goes to 9/11 so easily. It was such a big thing, and I lived through it, in that city that I was born in, and now I don't live in anymore. I'm sure those buildings gone has something to do with why I'm not there anymore. I remember that afternoon, being in Brooklyn, everybody was on the street, drinking, partying, a loud exodus of people on the bridge swarming into Brooklyn, like it was a snow day and school was cancelled. I don't think anybody knew anything. I didn't know. I remember getting on a bicycle and peddling around, and then feeling it necessary to bike into Manhattan, to see what had happened. I was peddling on the bridge, against the traffic of people who were walking, beers in their hands, drinking like it was Sunday. Some looked exhausted, some were bleeding, many of them laughed. It was exciting, like a parade. The ash under my tires was two inches deep, three as I got closer to the Manhattan side—it splashed up onto my back from the rear tire. Ash and paper, and that smell of burnt plastic, of people's bodies, but I didn't know that then. I probably had people's lives in my nose, literally the burnt bodies of people on my skin, in my nose, on my clothes. My friend John Creech, who has a set shop on Bond Street in Carroll Gardens, found a shoe and a desk calendar in front of his building. A shoe from three miles away. How did it get to the corner of Bond and McGraw streets in Brooklyn? What carried it there? For who to see? For John to find, to tell me that some mans shoe was in front of his door. I want to thank the man whose shoe that was. Whatever happened to him that morning, his shoe, on that street is a present my mind keeps and will not forget. I was standing on the corner of Vestry and Broadway on my bicycle at 4 P.M. on September 11th. Eleven minutes before the top of building number seven fell. Right there. I had biked up Vestry Street from Fulton. I passed a deli, one of the few down there, and stopped to look at the flowers out in the racks in front of the store. I remember they were those huge velvet red flowers that look like brains and they were covered in perfect piles of gray ash that just hovered undisturbed, balancing there like Calder mobiles. The compressor in the deli case hummed and standing 20 feet away, it had the most unnatural volume. Chris said he watched from his roof, and when the buildings fell, he said, there was a sheen in the air, like a metallic paint cloud, from all the glass breaking. Just a moment of metallic splinters suspended before the grumble of collapse. I remember that corner at 4 P.M., there were a bunch of firefighters crouched in front of me on the radio. The gray, soot sky dumped on us. They said I could go on, they weren't going to stop me, they had enough to worry about. They couldn't babysit me, or try to control me, or tell me what to do. Nobody has ever been able to tell me what to do. I once woke up out of a blackout from drinking sitting in a car that was spinning. I remember looking out the window as I slid and spun into the oncoming lane. I could see a truck's headlights in the windshield. The policeman told me I slid 100 feet, that I was hauling ass when I lost control. I remember waking up in the middle of it, spinning, the back of my head heavy like my neck was collapsing. I can imagine watching the car breeze past the front

21

of that truck, silently. As if the whole moment were paused, metal splinters waiting patiently. The car crashed into the stone foundation of an old house by the side of the road. I just missed that truck. What did I miss, did I lose something that night? That stone wall. My car broke a rock off it when it hit. One rock, a granite flagstone; like a shoe on a street, like a buoy in the ocean, a small reminder of a place in time

My mother wouldn't nurse me when I was born. She was only nineteen at the time. She had read something in some magazine saying that intimacy with a boy baby could lead him to being queer, gay, or homosexual. The term used in those days was queer. It seems that when I was quite young, and even when growing up, I was quite persistent in searching for my mother's affection. I can remember walking to a movie with her and reaching for her hand, which was refused to me. Also in my memory is that on Sunday mornings, I would lunge into her bed and again I would be told that I wasn't welcome there. I think she was always afraid I would come near her breasts, which were forbidden to me. The more she guarded them, the more I desired them. They were like the forbidden fruit in the Garden of Eden.

I always knew that my brother, older by almost three years, was my mother's favorite. He was handsome, brilliant, and finished Harvard Law School at the age of twenty. Nevertheless, I was constantly fighting for an equal place. I went into therapy for several years. The therapist told me that I have always been searching for her approval, but it always went to my older brother. Eventually, I knew I would be second place, and I was okay with that. I know that my mother meant well and that she loved me very much. She died three years ago.

I'm not a psychologist, but I have often wondered if the problems I faced as a child also affected me in later life. Several strange things occurred to me when I was an adolescent. But, the greatest problem that I had in those years was when all my friends had their voices deepen into manhood and mine remained the same beautiful boy's soprano. As a boy, I would have solos in the boy's choir in the Temple. However, when my voice remained soprano, it created huge problems for me. I was laughed at in high school. My dear father, of blessed memory, often scolded me at dinner saying, "Why don't you talk like a man?"

I tried everything I could think of to lower my voice. My mother took me to one doctor after another trying to cure the problem. See, she really cared for me; either that, or she was embarrassed by my childish voice. I went through all kinds of treatments. Nothing worked. I was a poor student in high school due to my self-consciousness about having to talk. I sat in the corner and never asked a question. I sulked around school, having only a few friends who didn't seem to mind my affliction. The more popular kids avoided me. I really don't know how I managed my life during those years. I spent two years in the army without incident and afterwards began a business where I was constantly talking to customers. Some of them made fun of me, but I was used to it. I would feel hurt inside, but would go on, as if nothing had happened. I wanted to tell them off, but business is business.

My business was very successful, so I had a lot pride in my accomplishment. Instead of going to college, I began working at the age of 21. I had a strong social life, not allowing my high-pitch voice to interfere with dating or going to parties. During my twenties, I was engaged three times. But, now I can't imagine what those girls were thinking or why they would enter into an engagement with me, or even go out with me. My last engagement was when I was 29. Married at 30, often I asked my wife how

23

she could marry me. She said it made her feel tenderness for my situation. Love is blind.

Finally, a famous voice doctor, Dr. Michael Cooper, met me when I was 43 years old. Within a period of six weeks of treatment, he had my voice drop to what it is today. When the doctor first picked up the phone and heard my voice, he said, "I can cure you. Come here at once." He insisted he could cure me. I explained that I had been to many doctors but they all failed. At that moment, he put a coin in his hand and insisted that I come for at least six sessions. He offered to treat me for double or nothing. His fees were rather high, and being frightened about the cost I agreed, but not double or nothing. I became his greatest success. He had me on his television show playing a tape of my old voice and then my new voice.

It has occurred to me that maybe, just maybe, my mother's behavior towards me when I was a child, might have brought these things on. Despite the answer, her memory is still beautiful to me. I loved her and I miss her very much.

On this island
there has been no place to hide.
My fear of what love drags with it
is cumbersome:

the endless togetherness,
the need to shave my legs,
to sleep in something not comfy-rag-ready,
to cook when I don't want to,
feeling guilty for being selfish,
having sex his way,
being polite,
being considerate,
controlling farts,
denying the gross.

Last night, after too much local rum,
we went down to the la palapa at the end of the dock
and sat,
our feet dangling in the water.

The night was a clumsy French kiss,
the water, black syrup.
The only lights were those at Roatan Ray's
on the other side of the bay.
The reggae music floated across the darkness.
No stars.
The sky misting that tropical rain
that doesn't feel like rain,
too bathtub warm.
We sat drinking chilled champagne,
The moisture plastered our clothing to our bodies
and melted the two us into one form.

He said, "I want to marry you."

The warm flow of alcohol charged to a low frequency sizzle.
My mouth went dry.
The four lights across the bay came into sharper focus.
I realized that the music had stopped.
A long frightened silence circled my ankles
and slithered up to my brain
where the synapses rapidly fired,

trying to file his statement of love.
Is it good news or bad?
Be careful.

I'm no spring chicken.
This may be my last chance,
my maybe last chance,
to not be a lonely old wither breasted woman
scuttling around an empty house
dusting chipped Roatan souvenirs
as reggae plays on the stereo.
Dusting mementos,
reminders of youth, of love, and possibility.

On this island
there has been no place to hide.

26

The driveway azaleas grow big as dogs and their stiff branches hunger for the touch of my car's glossy painted flanks. I see them arch, licking, stretching, wanting to hurt and own and eat.

But my car is no virgin. It loves rough trade, banged by grocery store carts that promise to call in the morning but never do, tattooed by the sharp keys of teenage night crawlers in the Rite Aid parking lot after midnight and, lets be candid, marred by my own careless kissing of curbs, rubbing tires against cement until the black rubber skin peels off as I parallel park with the kind of spatial perception which explains why I prosecute rather than paint for a living.

I do what is necessary to protect my own. I break the branches with my hands, muttering battle cries torn from Yeats—what rough beast is this, I say as I brace my hips against the car and lean hard into the azaleas. Or afterwards, my neck prickly with sweat, I survey my handiwork and say, with a tight smile, all is changed. Utterly changed. A terrible beauty is born.

But my own skin tears and blood pricks through. I sooth the stigmata of battle with my tongue and taste the salt and sap mixed together.

Each night, my car, like a bad teenage daughter, parks too close to danger, mocks my care and my love. It wants to live fast, die young and doesn't care about the body. And like an angry parent, I don't care what the stupid car lusts for. I know better. I know about loss and death and danger.

What does it matter to me if in order to avoid the rowdy branches I have to park too near the sprinklers, get wet nerdy splashes across the windows every fucking day? I don't care if I don't have the hard lacquered paint of other cars on the street. I don't have air fresheners and I never felt the lack. I don't sleep less well at night because I don't have vanity plates. But each morning, as I drive the car out of the driveway, away from the bushes, I know that I will come back at nightfall, that my headlights will rake across their hungry mouths and that I will surrender in the end to their dark embrace.

27

She rises in the night for cookies or candy,
with darkness around her
the walls sway and so does her ability to stay upright—
she falls with a crack; nasty cuts slice her forehead.
Blood on the doors tell a sketchy tale but leave no maps.
We know not, she knows not, for she can't remember.

Her left eye swells shut, two black eyes punch back
as you follow the deep purple bruises down her neck.
Hospital scans reveal a hematoma just under the bulbous bump.
The doctors and my father insist she stay,
though, she says, nay, but they triumph in the end.
Each moment of her two days kept, she is confusion and questions—
When can I go home? When can I go home? Why am I here?
She knows not, for she can't remember.

This particular fall, the worst, a trend over the last couple of years
of a failing body and mind so tired of its daily grind.
She used to repeat some words or phrases,
now it's constant, with no memory of moments before.
For the 14th time this hour, I answer the same question.
She eyes us suspiciously while guarding her red purse.
She accuses my father of sleeping with the supermarket checker.
And, we pray that the very next day she forgets these things
and that she won't remember.

Is this my fate, then?
When my night comes, will my mind be numb?
My intellect, seemingly dumb?
Having no knowledge of what I have become?

Worry? Yes, of course.
My father, still sharp as a tack, shipshape,
though he's had heart troubles over the years,
cannot fully take care of her.
I see him sway and wobble sometimes but he catches his possible
calamity in the nick of time, by wall or by will.

Why must it be this way? Is this God's kindness?
We come as babes and leave as babes
with our suitcase packed full of memories from our trip.

But, before we go, we open the suitcase

to reminisce and remember, till threadbare,
all those moments we held most dear or most painful.
We walk along well-worn carpet to show our children
or any one really, our prized pictures and figurines.

We tell them, those who will listen,
with stern knotted fingers pointing,
we tell them to prepare for old age.
A wearied warning to unseasoned travelers—
Stay away! Stay away!

Stay away from this place
if you can, they say,
I live here in this crumbling neighborhood
but would not wish it on my worst enemy.
But, now, who are you again?

She didn't ask for my advice.
At the end of a meeting
words slip from my lips
the way a glass falls
from my clumsy fingers.
My colleague looks blank,
then flashes unexpected anger
and walks away.
A bond has shattered,
not to be mended,
the unintended consequence of
my desire to do good.

I wish I could sweep up the syllables,
the way I do broken crystal,
and toss them in the trash.
Instead, I do inner penance.
It goes unseen,
yet gnaws like the tropical worm
that invaded my gut in Ecuador.

I writhe with discomfort
but don't say another word,
for fear that I'll do more damage.
Instead, I watch for signs
that what's been said
will finally evaporate
in the heat of daily life
and blow away in a fresh wind.

30

JUDI KAUFMAN **+ *I Am an Island***

Somewhere beyond
yesterday, today and tomorrow,
beyond our true or fake history,
is a wave in the vast ocean.

I'll meet you there
where the light shines.

JUDI KAUFMAN **+ *Legs Spread Wide***

The bottle sits before me on the bar.
Dark beer from Utah.
It's called Polygamy Porter.
The label says, "Why have just one?"

Picture one man, in loving color,
with seven women, legs spread wide.
As my Jewish grandmother would have said, "Vy haf just von?"

When I was 16 I screamed, I want to be an LDS.
A Latter Day Saint.
I want to be a Morman, I screamed.
Now I know why.
It's this bottle, this label.

The bottle is hard,
with a golden tip.
Under the light from the window,
it looks like a golden cock.
I drink it down in one swig.
The bartender come over.
"Gimmee another," I say.
"Why have just one."

The tables at this restaurant are unvarnished,
Or they were varnished but it is wearing off.
It's comfortable to me, this permissive erosion.
Perfection not required, inquire within.
My omelet is runny, the toast has blackened edges,
The potatoes are a little on the salty side.

My mother always sends things back.
She wants to live in houses that are new or only slightly worn.
A major remodel is acceptable as long as
All traces of previous life have been erased.

When we move into a new place,
I look for the edges of old wallpaper,
Unpainted spots in corners, initials carved in closets,
Assurances that people have thrived there before
And will thrive again.

Every embrace of the day is to be stretched into the blanket of night.
For it is there that the sharks, the tigers, and the hyenas may feed on you.
Hidden in dark night covered in your grossly slime of bad character.
Gone worse, gone wilder, gone hood.

For the no shows and the naysayers never offer a cloak.
Instead of a cover it is all black powder from the 45 shout down.
And the ropes that tie the injustice to the rails of the track,
They too need a rescue.
And the fat salmon gone lean can't find its way home again,
And I feel lost in the rain. The rain no longer bathes me
Nor washes yet away, the Sin, gladly festers.

And the children's chalk, hop scotch lost, its fine white powder
Worn thin on cocaine runs. Drugged out at day's end,
Screeching tires and honkys not in the race; no longer cool.

The hood becomes folded and the hood is the cloak,
The cloak of darkness where the tall trees and the pirate's hideout
Got lost in the tragedy of the real film.

"Hey you, watch it mother fucker, I'm gonna get yer ass
And yer gonna lose that Green yer flappin' round, real soon man,
Just roll over so I can run you over run you down real good, yeah,
That's right, get over there in that scramble and get yer mother fuckin'
Balls down to the wire never screechin' watch that steely blade,
No worn out baby here, yer born to lose and I ain't no savior
So get down or get goin'."

My, my! Red tide is up and grass is not green on the other side either.
And who wouldn't give a Buffalo nickel for a soda pop? You're wired.
And those of us in cages that you put us in! Oh my!
Who wouldn't want to pile into a '56 Chevy to a drive-in movie,
Order French fries with vinegar and neck the night away?

33

How did it get so twisted? When did the ball come down?
At midnight or at noon?
Right in front of us!
For it's goin' on around us.
In the foodstuffs, in the corporate corners,
In the Office of the Registrar, behind the desk at the bank.
A tall order to run right and play straight
When thieves wear stolen gold! Glorified!
When prices have challenged even themselves.
And the gravedigger leaves a trail at midnight, a trail of blood
To the "pass the buckers" all the way to the top.

Money covers money, good money after bad.
Just as any one can wipe away the slate or lose the records.
Depends on the color of your uniform,
"Who is the hero today may not be the hero tomorrow."

Mark my words and slip me a Mickey
If it don't see a dollar sign, what good is it?
That is the lament and it creeps of crap and dump trucks.
The track ain't clear. The race is fixed.
How do we hold today any decency
In the changing values of tomorrow?
Shall we trade civil rights for survival rights?
Humph!
You have to be flexible to run with the wolves.

34

Anthony A. Lee **+ *Father***

My mother threw my father
out of the house
when I was nine.
I visited him
on weekends
right up until I went to college.
But to him I
was always nine.
He could never get over
how much I had grown
that I could drive,
could write a proper check,
always asked me about girlfriends,
event though he knew
I didn't have one,
wanted to give me the talk
about the bees and birds,
but never got around to it.

His second wife said he
was a big kid
and stopped sleeping with him
after a few years.
His third wife did the same,
but he always had women
in between—

yes, anyhow, he bought a motorcycle once.
I think that was after
his second wife.
He was living in Pasadena.
I was at UCLA, a freshman.
When I drove up to visit,
he wanted to take me for a ride,
said he loved
the feeling of air
on his face,
the noise of the motor,
the smell of the gas,
and how you gun
the engine with your wrist,
not your ankle.

He had bought a black leather jacket
with steel studs, and he put it on.
He was pretty excited.

there was something tragic
about it, absurdly inane
adolescent glory finally strides forth, swaggering

That must have been my first time
on a motorcycle. I was sure
I was going to die.
There was nothing
to hold on to. So I
threw my arms around my father
and held on hard.

His sadness and mine tied
together at last,
cold air rushing,
motor screaming,
oil stinking,
wrists cranking.

I put my cheek
in the small of his back,
closed my eyes,
kept my arms locked
so I wouldn't fall—

and all the while thinking:
I love you.
I hate you.
I hate you.

Verbalize my inner sanctum
mumble jumble me
with wild thunder
jungle me wide
with tongue on lips
while hot coffee pot pulse
of cream on crusts
while the breath of me
clings by a clutch
to holy incantations
of this soil on flame.
Cause a girl
she's gotta live.
Some place
in her life
she's gotta have
a speck of land
that's her holy place.
Where the breath of her
is free
is free
to ooooh
to aaaaah.
Where the plump
of her thighs
can splish splash
against sea waves,
beat against skin cells
grown hot to the tremble.
It's a simple act
this transmigration of a rose
rising from nothing
to white embers on fire
to Mother Mary
and holy God
and all the while
the heart beat
rupturing from her deep,
the breadth of her
splayed on this bed,
a site for the sacred.

37

Wouldn't ya just know it? It's like I've been tellin' ya. When it rains, it pours. Just when I think things are gonna settle down they start to shake, rattle and scatter from point to point. Each point is separate, independent, isolated. Each point refuses to join harmoniously into a single flowing line.

Why do these points challenge me and every other Tom, Dick and Mary that wants to keep the pieces neatly arranged? It's like I've been tellin' ya. When it rains, it pours. Points surrounded by emptiness. Dark spots on a blank white page. Each point is marooned as an island. They should beg to be joined so they can become more than just a flyspeck that I want to rub out of existence.

I wonder why it is necessary to exist at all. I want to make my mark, but I don't want my mark to be a flyspeck. Part of me retreats. Part of me pushes forward. I want to be more. At the same time, I want to be less. I want my mark to flow into eternity. But my points want to scatter into the four winds.

Fear, worry, joy and happiness all seeking to occupy the same crowded space. That's me. A space. Just over there. On the green couch. Opposite the window. A space that is out of the sun but fanned into the flames of a glowing fire. Flames that stir the hearts of men, women and children. Flames that beat the drumbeat of life. Flames that smolder and turn everything into ashes.

Louder and louder, almost a whisper. A cry shattered into pieces, scattered into points beyond my control. Points that scatter through my life like buckshot from a rifle. How will I ever catch up? How will I ever complete anything? How will I ever get things arranged and put away? How will I ever bring order and design into this crowded joint where there just ain't no room to walk or move, let alone dance. It's like I've been tellin' ya. When it rains, it pours.

The day after was as bright and sunny as the day before. A perfect Indian summer day. We were all up around eight and everybody got to their bustling about. I think we had decided at that point that the party for her would be on Saturday. We were all orbiting each other in the kitchen, making or eating or cleaning up our breakfasts. We have been together in the kitchen like that in the morning plenty of times, during Christmas or Thanksgiving or any other family thing. You might have not even noticed straight away that my mother wasn't there.

Dad got up from the table. He had been writing some kind of list on the back of an envelope. He pushed back his chair and said, "So. I'm going to the funeral home."

You could feel the sentence register with all of us. This wasn't Christmas or Thanksgiving or any other family thing. It was our first day without her. And of course we all knew that, but you don't know it deep in your bones so soon after. It takes a long time to really know it and even then, you forget.

And besides, why should anything be any different? The kitchen had that same morning smell of shampoo and French roast and toasted bread, and behind it there was that cool morning smell that wafts in when deck door is open. My dad was wearing a black t-shirt and black cords, and I didn't know if he had meant to do that or not. With him, it could have been totally unconscious. He hadn't shaved, either. Which was strange. Because in the morning his face is smooth and his skin glows. But apart from those things, everything was the same — same good clear September sunlight, same coffee mugs, same little cereal bowls, same napkins on our same kitchen table. My nephew Will was strapped into the high-chair, every bit the beautiful boy he ever was, with his blond hair standing almost straight up on the top of his head. We were just us having breakfast. My mom could have easily been showering downstairs. My dad could have just as easily said he was going down the hill to run any errand at all.

So I did what I always do. I volunteered.

"I'm coming with you," I said. "Let me just grab a sweater."

In Kindergarten, we all had crushes on Bradley Obermyer. Twelve of us.

Bradley was a bland boy. We were too young to be attracted to the bad boys, the James Dean types. At that age, the boys who were "bad" were still just "gross". They hadn't yet become so bad we wanted them. Bradley was blonde and actually fairly nice, as I recall, though I can't remember a single moment I spent with him. I do, however, still have a postcard I wrote to him from San Diego, on a cross-country trip with my family. We had been that day to the San Diego Zoo. In our hotel room, the over-bright California sun had started to go down, and the pinky sunset color was seeping through the windows and sending shafts of light filled with dancing dust particles across my hotel bed. I am sitting cross-legged in my pink Keds and powder blue shorts, surrounded by all my postcard choices, spread out on the anonymous blue carpet. I pick up the one with two striped tigers and hold it close to my tiny face. They sit together, the tigers, majestically facing out to the camera, a couple. This is the one.

I turn it over and place it on the floor in front of me, and pop the cap off the Navy Blue Magic Marker.

"Bradley," I begin. My whole little body is bent down into the act of writing, when it took a whole body to make a sentence, to make a word. My family is in the adjoining room, my brothers voice chattering, telling little known facts he'd discovered about the zoo, about the eating habits of giraffes or something. Here in this room, the Zoo has become unimportant. It is all Bradley, all the time.

"Bradley," I continue, "You are as strong as a tiger." I carefully spell out the five letters of my name, crooked in the Little white space since there are no lines to guide my hand. Then I choose another. This one is a Zebra, black and white, like the tiles on the floor of my grandmother's building.

"Bradley," I write again, "I miss you."

There was only one Bradley, and twelve of us who loved him to distraction, who giggled about him from the four-square court. So he decided, to be fair, to marry all of us. But his favorite, and he was clear on this point, was Molly Dean. So she would be his major wife, with all the rest of us below her on pretty much the same level. We'd all live together in a big house, we decided, or maybe on a farm. I was happy to be included as one of Bradley's wives. I hid the fact that I was jealous of Molly—what was the point? A twelfth of Bradley was better than no Bradley at all. Today, lying in bed as my husband dreams beside me, splayed out and taking up probably more than his half, I still can't get over that he has chosen just me to marry. With me, that goes a long way. Take that, Molly Dean!

By first grade, the blush on the rose had faded, and Bradley Obermyer was no longer our dream future. Those must have been his Glory Days, those Kindergarten months when twelve girls were happy just to be allowed to share him as a husband. By first grade, it was the boys who called us names who became attractive, the ones who left dead bugs in our cubicles and chased us and scared us. The ones who took our small comforts, our security blankets, our dolls, and hid them or threw them over our heads to each other, or who stole our folded-up private messages, and read them aloud and humiliated us, these boys became our secret desires. Our "Dear Diary" scribbled longings. The boys they would eventually grow into would be the ones we'd have to get over, the ones we'd think we couldn't live without, the ones who'd keep us waiting and break our hearts. Molly Dean would become a lesbian and move to Rhode Island.

I would find the Bradley postcards from the Zoo years later, unsent. I never had his address.

In the most common and everyday existence of couples, there is something dramatic and remarkable.

I see them, and like us so many times, completely in it. You said they were alcoholics. They live hard and play hard and live completely inside that intensity. There are no surprises, this is who they are. They reveal their psychological depth, not idealized but somehow rendered heroic.

She, in her best Sunday clothes, he, his lit cigarette and working class forearms. That is their own, yet where their bodies touch—it becomes them. It is soft, tender, her hand rests in his arm. Somehow, one knows he will never leave her. He is all man, like you my king, he is all that to her. He doesn't need to be anything for her and he knows it.

They don't know how to hold each other safely or fully, or live past today, because more than love, they possess a primal need and an insatiable hunger and a lust to feed off each other's wounds. One will die without the other, or so they believe. Even though there is a lot of shouting, she will have his dinner waiting for him when he comes home. His work clothes will be mended, washed and ironed. The nicer shirts will hang from the shower rod. They will sleep together nightly and in the morning she will prepare his coffee.

There is no sign on her body
that says Caution.
Out of Order.
Chemical Imbalance.
No theory of quantum physics
explains the distance
between where she is
and the smile she wears;
explains an absence of feeling
so vast
it laughs in the wings
as she flubs her lines,
forgets to smile on cue.

Ask me
if there is mental illness
in my own family,
and I'll say no.
I don't count my depression,
or family therapy
or individual therapy.
I don't count my step-kids
or my uncles, aunts, cousins.
I won't name the ones
who were drug-dependent or bipolar
or shell-shocked or schizophrenic.
I forget all about the eating-disordered,
the senile, the homeless,
the incarcerated, the suicidal.
I remember them as
students with promise,
musicians, chefs,
teachers, engineers,
stock brokers, cashiers,
gas jockeys, mommies,
daddies.
I remember them as
the dear children
and the damned ones.

They're as common as blades of grass
that break through the asphalt,

43

or crows that chatter from the rail
on the neighbor's deck.
It's as common as Mom on the couch
with a headache,
Dad working late again tonight,
or the dog gnawing at
the bare skin on his left flank.

How long can parents hold their breath?
Till the pregnancy is confirmed,
till the fingers are counted,
till the first steps are taken,
till the first words are spoken,
till the doctor says this is normal,
till the doctor says this is not,
till the first medication takes effect,
till the next medication,
till the hope is all gone,
till the smile returns,
till the diploma's received,
till the vows are exchanged,
till the grass cuts through the asphalt,
till the crows stop mocking.

Elaine Mintzer's debut poetry collection, **Natural Selections,** *appeared in 2005 as a Bombshelter Press publication. She was born in Los Angeles. Elaine received a BA in Creative Writing from UCLA and an MS in Education from USC. Her work has been anthologized in* **13 Los Angeles Poets**. *Ms. Mintzer wrote poetry for, and read with the performances of the dance company Ballet Randolph in Miami Beach. She lives with her family in Manhattan Beach, CA, and teaches at a nearby high school.*

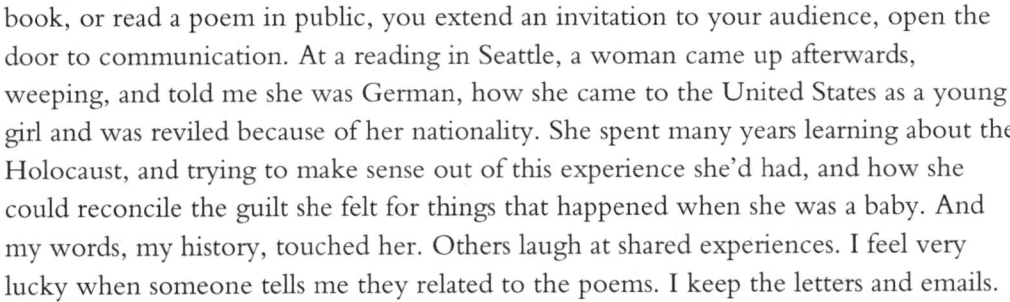

VW: What do you like best about having written this book?

EM: It's been gratifying to hear how my words affect others. Any time you write a book, or read a poem in public, you extend an invitation to your audience, open the door to communication. At a reading in Seattle, a woman came up afterwards, weeping, and told me she was German, how she came to the United States as a young girl and was reviled because of her nationality. She spent many years learning about the Holocaust, and trying to make sense out of this experience she'd had, and how she could reconcile the guilt she felt for things that happened when she was a baby. And my words, my history, touched her. Others laugh at shared experiences. I feel very lucky when someone tells me they related to the poems. I keep the letters and emails.

Of course, the communication is not always positive. One acquaintance felt compelled to give me a lesson in observation and ornithology because she didn't agree with one poem. One of my best friends told me the poems made her feel uncomfortable; that they addressed areas and feelings she preferred to avoid. Now she carries my book with her on business trips, and tells me how much my story is her story.

VW: *Natural Selections* is divided into seven sections. How did you come up with a plan for the organization?

EM: Chapter breaks do for my book what line breaks and stanza breaks do for the poems. Breaking the book up made me look at themes, time periods, subjects—all the elements that define the writing—and make choices. There were so many ways to organize, and each way emphasized a different aspect of the writing. I looked to Charles Darwin for inspiration, because of the title I'd chosen, and I'm happy with the results.

VW: Who has influenced your poetry?

EM: When I was young, my dad borrowed a book of poetry from the public library. It was over a thousand pages, and I could barely pick it up. He let me sit on his lap and look at the poems. He read them to me, mostly the Romantics, Keats, Shelley, Yeats, Coleridge. He made sure I understood the words, and he tried to get me to understand the deeper meanings, but alas, I was a little girl.

In college, I had a wonderful course at UCLA with Stephen Yenser, who introduced me to Pound, Eliot, Berryman, Wilbur, Roethke, Plath and Hughes.

And over the last 16 years, I've been studying with Jack Grapes, who invites his writers to immerse themselves in writing with abandon and with purpose, to rip the edges off the pages and their self-imposed constraints. He also has a fine eye and ear for editing.

VW: Writing is such a solitary activity. How do you overcome that?

EM: Luckily, my life and my work are full of people. But writing is hard when it's always alone. For the past twenty years or so, my best friend has been my writing partner, and we support each other through dry times and all the self-recriminations that come when no one else is around to comment about your work. I've been part of the L.A. Poets and Writers Collective, taking writing classes and participating in editing groups. I've made incredible contacts in the community for poetry that's been commissioned; poetry for a ballet in Miami, where I was welcomed into the world of dance and theater, and a poem for the National Alliance for the Mentally Ill for a fundraiser in Seattle.

VW: A lot of people would like to write a book. How did yours get done?

EM: I applied for a sabbatical from teaching for the purpose of writing the book. I didn't want to go back to work the following September with nothing to show for my year. I'm tremendously proud of my accomplishment, because the alternative of just having fun and wasting time was always there.

Most of the poems were written in the years before my sabbatical. I took the time to really edit. Even though I've been editing work for years, there was something I really understood by doing this big job. When we write, the picture and the meaning are clear in the author's head. The trick is making sure it is clear to the reader. Each line should be as smooth as it can be. It should say exactly what you want it to say. The trouble is, that's hard, and it takes time. I gave myself nine months to edit my poems, and permission to let them be good enough at the end of that time. There were a handful of poems that got cut at the end because they had problems I haven't figured out how to solve.

VW: The book has a strong spiritual theme that runs through the poems. Are you a religious person?

EM: I am Jewish. I was the first girl to be Bat Mitzvahed at my synagogue when I was thirteen. I spent a year working on a kibbutz in Israel, and studying, and continued studying and teaching in synagogues when I was in college. And I have spent my adult years avoiding organized religion. That doesn't mean I don't have the same longings and questions as everyone else. I think all poets are, by virtue of the kinds of observations they make about the world, spiritual and political.

I believe in the religious powers of poetry. When my daughter was a year old, she and I flew home on a prop-jet from Lake Tahoe, while my year-old son drove home with my husband. I've never been fearful about flying, but I sat there weeping with my daughter in my lap as the plane taxied down the runway. All I could think of was a poem my dad made me memorize a long time ago, "Requiem," by Robert Louis Stevenson.

> *Under the wide and starry sky,*
> *Dig the grave and let me lie,*
> *Glad did I live and gladly die,*
> > *And I laid me down with a will.*
>
> *This be the verse you grave for me:*
> *Here he lies where he longed to be,*
> *Home is the sailor, home from sea,*
> > *And the hunter home from the hill.*

There ain't no hope, ain't there? Ain't no skin that can hold these guts and bones, ain't no sieve for my dreams to drip through and puddle on the bottom of the pan. The dog licks my feet; I should be licking his! The owl hoots from the dark wire—it's a perch for her. Can she feel the conversations buzzing through her talons? Or is she preoccupied by the heartbeats of a mouse? Hotel blues, dull distant roar of late night traffic on the nearby Interstate. Alone in my hotel room. I am alone with my thoughts and my sensations. I am alone, and lonely, trying to breathe this stagnant air. Where are the fireflies? It is summer, the dog days of Illinois. There were fireflies here when I was a boy, dancing through the evening mist of a warm wet field, blinking with cold light, illuminating me with their mysterious code. My tongue is thick and speechless. The soundtrack of a horror movie drifts from the drive-in screen in the hotel parking lot—an old John Carpenter classic, *The Fog*, if I remember correctly. I am stuffed with salmon ($60 for dinner!), stuffed with Bill, and the air in here is heavy and dead. My cat is dead; my father is dead; my mom is 88 (at least). She would never tell us her age (don't make me old, she'd say), but I glimpsed her birth date on some document or other. How did I get so old? Why am I still so young? Maybe my best work is behind me. Maybe I'm not really here. I'd like to be an animal prowling the green belt across the street from this hotel, prowling through the bushes and the trees, sniffing the broken glass and dirt for tasty deer and chipmunks and plump raccoons. I'm ready to sink my fangs through mammal fur into mammal flesh, ready to bellow my victory to the other creatures in my domain. My God, we've gotten old! The wrinkles beneath my eyes! This belly full of carrot cake and macadamia nut ice cream! These white hairs! Be gone, age! Depart, you whispers of doom! Let me run through the trees, hell, straight up the trunks, fifty feet up and out across the branches, springing off the bending boughs and catapulting through the sweet night air, through swarms of fireflies, through time itself, to splash into the muddy, sad Des Plaines River, the mighty roaring Des Plaines River, chancred by white plastic buckets & root beer-colored foam. Thirty-foot carp with tremendous sucker mouths await my command. I stand astride the scaly backs of two enormous fish, hold the reins in one hand, crack my whip with the other, and steer them all the way home to mom.

48

the men I serve by day are gluttonous and
sunburned and make me feel small,
the type of poor creature who physically breaks
easily,
these men who I do not trust. perhaps

they were once young, perhaps,
and if they were, I would have hated them
as they felt shame in front of friends after
having expressed a feeling too emphatically,

a mind with no meat and all fat, lard-headed,
sunburnt, gluttonous men that I serve by day.
I take revenge by eating fries from their plates.
perhaps they know.
they know

that I am small. that I am young, that I will
break easily
and have never had to learn about how to survive
physical force.

actually, it is just one of them.
one of these men that I serve is twice my height
and four times my width,
a giant,
he makes me imagine men who make laws that make
good wives out of women,
this fucking hulk of a human blister makes me
think of lawmakers.

I struggle
to open
the window
in my bedroom that faces the Pacific,
it is behind me as I lay here in bed alone and so
I make a kind of
awkward curve
of my arm, an impossible curve in fact, that makes
me struggle
to slide so simple a pane.
there is nothing outside but primordial stew,
did you know that ocean water tastes like a man?

demure and childish, I
often forget what is appropriate and flirt too
much and make demands,
both are nervous habits, I wonder what kind of
woman I'll make,
I wonder if I will ever love like thick skin and
be like weather.

oh who cares?
who cares
about a small girl
who despises men who are like
alien tourists in this world,
crunching aluminum cans and giggling about sex.

this is not work, I realize.
this is a lesson I have been assigned to learn
as the new girl on the block.
school is out, what you think is nothing. I am
your business, your rent, your day,
these are my orders,
obey.

It's always the mother.
The beating of her heart
sounded through my being
as if it were mine.
Its rhythmic predictability and resolve
lulled me to an intoxicating stupor.

When I emerged from her distant lands—
when she received me in her flesh—
I wonder what soulful knowings
And wistful feelings seeped into me
while submerged in her dark life currents.

I wonder if I bathed
in her motherly warmth
or did I sink into her secret unworthiness?
They say that lack of primal love moves
like a contagious disease
and infects all hopeful lovers.

Once I was released into life—
at what moment did I realize the difference
between my heart beat and hers?
What was in her gaze
when she first met mine?

My heart's chambers fill, empty, and fill again.
But I am not graceful with the rhythms of life—
when to let things die
and when to birth and find renewal.

I shuddered and convulsed
when floods took the imagined
too-good mother away.
I could no longer find protection
in the suffocating nest and the too-safe life.

It's always the mother.

How do I find my vision, when all I see
I see through her eyes?
I lived inside her wound.
We sat through many tearful car rides.
I mirrored her cares and concerns.

51

This is not me, Mother, it's you.
See, I can be just what you want me to be.
For a while I knew her better than myself.
But that side of me died a long time ago.

I don't want to exploit my rebellious nature—
To be in opposition just to be different.
But I want to go beyond the confines of her life,
beyond the confines of her ways of suffering.
There were so many ways of suffering,
and I learned them all.
Yet, a deep sense of betrayal and guilt
lingers with every renunciation.
It's always the mother.

We shared a dressing room together, my mother and I.
She now struggles to change her clothes.
Arthritis and pain have left their traces in her contracted face.
I kneel by her foot to help her tie
her unfashionable orthopedic shoes.

I kneel before her.
Her gray hair is no longer camouflaged with blonde highlights,
as if looking happy were no longer a priority.
I kneel before her
and wonder how many more dressing rooms will we share?
My heart fills with love and loss,
Because I knew the intimate
beating of her heart
long before mine.

Mother, it's always the mother.
And now it has finally come to this, Mother.
It is my turn to be the mother.

He looks like crap,
my ex.
He's pasty and fat.

When I had him,
he was an Adonis.
He worked out.
He ate food
between the bottles—

Now, it's probably just
Bottle and then bottle and then cigarettes.

No woman to say,
"Smoke that shit outside."

No woman to say,
"What would you like for dinner?"

No woman to say,
"I love you."

It was nighttime at the Mateel Community Center—Day three of our escape to Reggae on the River. Four of us lay there on our backs soaking in the night sky from some spot on the festival grounds. We were far enough from any city that no light or pollutants obstructed our view and it seemed like all the stars had come out to play.

This one star in particular caught my eye and I started staring at it obsessively. It was at the tip of this arrow formed by a few other stars, but something about it called out to me. It was the shimmer, just a little different than all the other ones and I swore by everything that was true to me that I was communicating with it: that it was trying to communicate with me. That's when Steve spoke.

"The stars are so beautiful," he said. "And I got one all picked out."

Steve was lying down right next to me, wearing his dirty flannel over some t-shirt and baggy shorts tattered around the edges. I wasn't dressed much different: old cargo pants with a nice sized chunk missing from the left pant leg. But I had on a heavy sweater that made for a nice added cushion on the soft grass.

All of us had been drinking and smoking weed all day out in the open with fifteen thousand other pot-heads, listening to reggae. And like a good portion of those people, we'd been popping ecstasy like Advils for the last three days and chewing on mushrooms like they weren't bad for you. I guess it's no surprise I was feeling spiritual—and my guess is Steve was feeling it too. Who wouldn't? We were young, high, and hallucinating in the wilderness, the cool night air fresh and cleansing our spirits.

Somewhere, not too far away, there was a stage where some band was pumping good vibes at us. All the food stands and little booths selling beads and henna tattoos and vegan brownies had closed down for the night. But I couldn't see any of that: couldn't see the red and yellow and green banners flapping in the breeze, couldn't see the couples that I'm sure were dancing somewhere nearby. I couldn't even see Steve and his scrawny little body and long hair and Jesus looking face. All I could see was that star—but I could feel everything else. I could feel it in my bones and in my skin and in my hair and in my fingers. Something about that feeling made me know Steve was looking at the same star I was. Sure the arrow was pointing at it, but to me it seemed like the whole sky was pointing at it. And then I was pointing at it.

"Is it that one?" I asked him.

Steve nearly lost it. He jumped higher than I've ever seen a man jump from a lying position and landed on his side asking me how in the hell I knew that. But how could I not? The whole sky was pointing at it.

Today I realize that Steve might have thought I was pointing at a different star altogether. Mushrooms and a blurred finger under a big sky have a strange way about them, after all. But that's no matter. That night I communicated with the universe—and I think Steve did too.

I look through a window pane witnessing
blue skies painted with grey-white clouds,
a terra cotta building.

Inside my heart I am troubled with the past,
feel one way think another, do my best.

Contemplate, as clouds float by
is this authentic?

Inside there is a fire burning,
yearning a deeper connection to feel harmony.
Ice cream, hiccups, cell phone rings, a friend from New York, lives are separate
hearts connect, phone disconnects. Hello . . . Hello . . . HE-LLO?

The earth is moving,
the clouds stay the same,
my mood spins,
I want to sleep,
but I sit writing.
The thought of tea sounds good right now as my
tongue presses up on the roof of my mouth.
I take a deep breath only to feel the clouds in my lungs
exhale—my ribs feel achy, the clouds shift.

My eyesight in my left eye is distorted
I digest the blurry views but there is clarity in my right.
My body feels a storm coming from within my being.

My skin gets tight when I am not being true.
Filled with fear the truth desires to be free.
Skin like Saran Wrap being pulled tight but my truth wants to leak out.
It begins to hiss as it gets tighter, the pores of my skin begin to leak my essence,
this time I cannot hide.

Authenticity, a question,
what is it to YOU?
ME? Well it's better to fail as who I am and not try to become someone else.
I learned this the hard way and see it as a waste of time.

Figure it out for your-SELF.
Even if your skin begins to tighten,
eventually it will peel, shed like a boa constrictor revealing your TRUE self.
Even if it pains you, there will be a relief, a sigh of relief to see that YOU have arrived.

Together let's wear our skin with the utmost respect admitting that it's borrowed.
Eventually, to be left behind, given back to the source from whence it came.

Back to the dust that make the stars that are in the blue sky,
back behind the white clouds past the terra cotta building,
simply, waiting to shine as them-SELVES comforted in the blanket of the night.

"You know, Jackie, I really enjoy being with you."

La Vie En Rose was pretty crowded, but we were in a booth near the back, away from the swinging doors to the kitchen, so it felt private. Our own little world.

It was our third date, and I liked him. A lot. He'd picked the restaurant again, which was fine with me. He had good taste. We could've been at Mickey D's for all I cared, but it was fun to sit at a table draped in stiff white linen, with flickering candlelight reflected in my wine glass and soft classical music playing in the background.

Our waiter had a convincing French accent and had served our salads with a flourish and a wink at me. Little red and yellow tomatoes glistened in a bed of bright greens, just waiting to be speared by chilled forks.

We had really clicked, I thought, just like my friend Mary promised when she set us up. And I was so relieved—it had been a long, sad time since my last relationship self-destructed. I was ready.

And there he was: nice looking, tall, early 40s, just like me. So what if his hair was beginning to thin a little and he could stand to lose maybe ten pounds. Heck, so could I for that matter. My hair didn't show its age thanks to a really good colorist in Pasadena who kept the brown looking natural.

He tended to dress up a little more than I was used to; that night he had on a crisp white shirt and a gray sport coat over navy trousers—never jeans, I don't think he owned any. No tie, although he'd worn one on our first date. I sort of liked the way he dressed, even if it meant I had to wrestle myself into panty hose and high heels when I'd have been more comfortable in pants. But he'd taken me to the opera on our first date, a chamber music performance on our second, and that night we were going to a play, so I'd thought, better safe than sorry as I zipped up the third of my basic black dresses, the one he hadn't seen yet.

He loved to talk, and I loved to listen. He was really well informed—I think he read the daily paper all the way through. He could give you the scoop on which politician was in trouble this week, why the stock market was still a good bet, when housing prices were going to level off, where to find a good deal on a car, and how to negotiate the best price. So I was pretty taken by him, all right, and I'd been happy that he kept asking me out.

His eyes were dark and unreadable in the candlelight, but he was smiling at me, smiling like he meant it. His right hand rested on the table, and I knew if I reached out and touched it, which I very well could do, his skin would be warm and welcoming.

I put down my fork. "Julie," I said. "My name is Julie."

I am on the verge of something big
about to enter a new place, ascend to another level.
The sound of a new fountain
in the background, a wellspring.
One surgery and no more contact sports.
Beloved escape vanished
under the surgeon's knife.
A second surgery and I can no longer run.
Mad women run in my family.

Not anymore they don't.
Madwomen.
Nanny ran away from six children.
Grandma ran away from her husband.
Mom ran away from her stepfather.
Mad women run.
I ran up and down the coast.
I ran to L.A. until the sum of my weaknesses
boarded together into strength
to raise my kids. I stopped running.
Madwomen no longer run in my family.

I can pinpoint the moment
sitting on a bench at the edge
of a canyon looking out at the city
with my daughter leaning against me.
In front of us yellow flowers against blue sky
the weight and warmth of her leaning
against my side formed
one of those memories that will sustain her.
Madwomen no longer run in my family.

She will remember the colors,
how she wanted a photograph of the tree branches
against the sky blown up
to decorate the ceiling of her room
and that when she feels crazy and overwhelmed
she will remember that we stopped
and she came back to herself.
Mad women run.

I told her madwomen no longer run in our family
and then a bee heavy with pollen flew

from the flowers off to the hive.
change came from joy instead of pain.
Clarity more than change.
And it was very much like lighting a candle.
I struck a match and moved it to the wick
watching the magic of fire transferring
from one to the other in an instant
and that is what happened in the quiet
beneath birds calling and bees working.
I strike to hit like a hammer or a fist.
Like lightning after thunder.
The warning and the illumination.
To make a space or strike out
She is not the only one who was ignited
on that mountain bench
I was struck like a match.

Growing up in Japan,
my sisters and I,
we loved rainy days.

Walking down the road
to our elementary school,
red school backpacks
and umbrellas at hand,
we loved rainy days.

Rainy days meant
cover-up days.
Cover up our faces
with our little umbrellas.
'Cause if, God forbid, we showed
our foreign-looking faces,
the whole wide world would scream
at our faces,
pointing fingers and mocking faces,
shouts of *gaijin* all the way home.

But rainy days were
blessings from above,
a little short break in our little heartaches.
Rainy outside but shiny inside,
unlike those other days
that it rained inside.

My sisters and I—
we loved rainy days.

Zippy words, normal words
Zippy words, normal words
Accelerated sentences, normal sentences
Accelerated sentences
Seeing ghosts, seeing reality, seeing ghosts
Hearing people, really hearing people, hearing people
Light and airy
Lots of color

Zippier zippy words, zippier zippy words only
Accelerated broken sentences, accelerated broken sentences only
Seeing multiple ghosts, seeing multiple ghosts everywhere
Hearing many people's voices
Hearing many people's voice everywhere

Zippy, visions, voices, color everywhere
Zippy everything, accelerated everything, visions everywhere
Continuum

Zippy, speedy, voices, faces, real, surreal
Zippy, speedy, voices, faces
Just zippy

Flat, black, bleak, heavy silence
Paranoid languid voices
Seeing death

Hearing paranoid attacking voices within me
Suffocating darkness

Catatonic sleepy yawning Continuum
Day after day sleeping
Not even seeking for life and voices
Fading

Monotone everything, slow to a halt everything, visions of ending here no vision of
    there
Monotone everything, slow to a halt everything, visions of ending here no vision of
    there
No zippy desire or option
Why stay

Black, bleak, dark, gray today
Black, bleak, dark, gray tomorrow

Why bother

Spurts of pastel color, no Fauvism or motion
Flowers appear to be flowers
Awake in
Slow motion

Life in black and gray

Memories of zippy horrify
Medicated cadenced words
Visions become views from the widow
Voices are staccato caretaker concerns
Pendulum balanced

So, get a load of this,
I overheard this woman talking about how if you haven't had sex in seven years,
you are technically a born-again virgin.
I guess it takes seven years for it to get all good and tight again.
If I had a nickel for every guy I'd like to erase from my vagina,
I'd have fifty cents.

Born again virgin, it has got a nice ring to it.
"Why buy the cow if you're getting the milk for free?"
my Mom used to say to me.
So many damn types of milk,
Whole, 2%, 1%, non-fat, soy, rice, almond.
Life used to be simple,
you like a guy, he likes you, you flirt, you kiss, yada yada yada,
you're spending seven hours on your bedroom floor
making mix tapes filled with cheesy love songs.
I poured blood, sweat and tears into those frickin' tapes—
that's how I knew when I was in love.
So they got my milk and my music.

So, cut to—now, this second,
I've got milk, and I've got music,
but somehow I'm on my way to joining Mary, God bless her virginal soul.
Too many choice of milk, and too many lactose intolerant men.
What if Starbucks is to blame for EVERYTHING?
I mean, with a frickin' Starbucks on every god damn corner,
how's a lovely ladylike me supposed to find true love?

63

MEWS SMALL **+ *Sirens***

—by an American peacemaker

I can't stop thinking about the sirens careening through the streets everywhere.

All around the world . . . all those that come . . . and all those that do not. Because there are no sirens, no ambulances, no fireman to save all that is burning.

We said, no. But they spent all of our money on killing machines and on our weapons of mass destruction.

What about all those needing help all around the world? And all those that desperately need, but never call. What about all those people? So hopeless they do not even know there is help. There are helpers always, everywhere, but often they are not seen. I know they are here, I see them all the time and they come in infinite forms. I see them standing right in front of wounded souls that are crying out. I see them not seeing the specialist doctor that is right there, for them. Perhaps it is because the doctor has no degree or wears some other uniform. Could be the guy who is parking your car or the bus driver or the cashier at the market or the homeless vet on the corner asking you for food, money or work, or the one who is not asking for anything . . . just there out there on the street somewhere, deep in their soul hoping you will see them and give them a helping hand or just acknowledge them. Looking deep into another soul, being there fully can heal your own sorrows.

But, what about the war zones, where there is poison everywhere and hundreds and thousands are dying? I have not lived in Bosnia, Rwanda, Iraq or any of the countries all around the world that are still fighting.

Still they are fighting. What can be done? How to stop? Are we ready to stop? Are we ready to hear, to listen, to give and receive? To not agree, but to remain still, to forgive. And feel for solutions. Solutions are there!

Yes! I am ready! Does each human being need to be ready? How many does it take? I don't know. Could it happen quickly like the Domino Effect in reverse?

Yes, I stand up for life and then another. And another, another, then a whole field of people, then a whole country.

And then the whole world!

Now. Let's have it now, right now, everywhere, all around the world, peace now.

Sirens. We can be sirens. I am declaring, right now, I am a siren for peace, careening through the streets of my life and the veins of my being reverberating through the universe now for peace, not tomorrow but today. Now!

Your love
permeates
all parts
of me
skin
tissue
muscle
down deep
into
my bones
flows through
my veins
into
every cell
into
the very molecular structure
of me
into
the atom
my body breaks down to be
and then on
into
my soul.

Another visit to Pasadena. That's where my dentist resides. Hovers above the city looking for those dam fillings, cavities, and worst of all, root canals. There are so polite, the helpers smile with their white teeth and say, "Welcome, so good to see you again." All I could hear is the door slamming behind me with the velocity of a train going down the tracks towards its destination. I sit in the waiting room, such a nice atmosphere—magazines of Tom Cruise, with his dam crooked white teeth smiling at me, taunting me. I hear Frank Sinatra singing, "I did it my way," and I sit there wondering how deep the drill is going to go into my bloody gums. Give me the Listerine, give me the dental floss, give me a machine that will fix my teeth. O, I am so sorry, I neglected you, shunned you, let you rot under my grinding nervousness. Sleep, sleep, O blessed sleep, that's where the most destruction was being done, those evil angels that come out in the darkness, move my teeth, shake the very ground that they lie on. Erosion has led me to this chair that overlooks the pretty city of Pasadena. They warned me, said I would have problems when I get older, damn them, they were right, and now I stand before you pleading for mercy.

"Hi Jack, how are you?" Dr. Murdock asked.

Murdock, the son of a great dentist, his father was a master. Finished first in his class at USC. A long line of patients have come into this office to see the master, not the student, but the master is now dead, all the accolades have been spoken. The untested son has taken over the operation and has the audacity to ask me a silly, asinine question pertaining to my state of mind.

"I'm fine, thanks" I said.

I could see the drills panting with anticipation of upcoming events. The dogs are downstairs snarling with their sharp teeth, growling, biting, itching to be released into the mouth of blood and decay. Of broken childhood dreams that have been destroyed. Oh, that hurts, you bastard, give me the novocaine, anything to numb my memories of this horrible happening in the city of Pasadena.

"Well Jack, you need a root canal," Murchian said.

Traitor, villain, you are a poor imitation of your great father. Blood has been shed and now the death toll will be tallied. This one thing you should know, no matter how much it cost, I will have me revenge on all of you hacks, you rich boys who destroy the very gum line that X-rays said were fine six months ago.

"How much is it going to cost?" I asked

"I'll let my assistant come in and go over everything with you" Murdock said.

Coward, the sun is breaking through the shutters and exposing your character. Run, run away, run back to your study hall, I'll remain here in the foxhole with the blood and my fellow comrades.

It was a costly day for me. Lots of dollars and cents for a tooth that nobody will see. Another childhood memory has fallen. With each tooth that is replaced by a phony one, I lose a part of my past. That little boy who was standing on the rail, by the docks, the boats swaying back and forth, the crabs performing their daily chores, the chlorine filled pool waiting for my arrival, the photo is becoming fainter and fainter, farther and farther away with every wicked drilling that takes place. I will fight for that picture, my

66

teeth are part of my body, this hideous battle will be fought from the bathroom, not with guns, but with dental floss, electric toothbrushes, and a mouth piece to keep my memories still, still in my mouth so I'll be able to remember who I am.

67

I loved it when my mother would tell me to bring a dish of macaroni up to Mrs. Weiss. It was four flights up and past Mrs. Goldberg's who we were all convinced gave out poison apples on Halloween. Inevitably, she would always open the door just as I would pass and say, "Oh, hi Carol, I thought it was Pauline! " Well, she knew it wasn't Pauline. She was always fighting with Pauline. But she knew it wasn't Pauline. She just had to stick her head out and see who it was, she just had to know everybody who went to see Mrs. Weiss. She was like Mrs. Weiss' gate keeper. She was everybody's gatekeeper. I hated having to go past her door, but Mrs. Weiss was great and it was worth all the obstacles to go upstairs and see her. She always had a new lesson for me about something or another. I learned a lot from her. About the World. Mainly Europe and Germany and how beautiful it had been. Sometimes the lesson would be about history or the news of the world that day. And sometimes it was about religion. She never spoke to me like I was seven. Like a child. She talked to me smart and clear like I was her friend. I never got the spiritual guidance in Catholic School that I got from Mrs. Weiss. She taught me so much about Judaism and the prophets, Elijah and Jesus, that I toyed with the idea of converting so that I could meet Elijah.

Whenever I walked into her two-room apartment, there would always be biscuits on the table and she'd be making tea. She didn't have a telephone. How did she know I was coming? I lived for the biscuits as well as the objects and "chatchkas" that filled the room. She had a story for every one of those things, her little "chatchkas," as she called them. And the ones that didn't have a story, well, I would make a story up myself. What you must know about Mrs. Weiss is that she never went out. All she could do was stay at home and make dolls, the most beautiful handmade wooden dolls you've ever seen. I was her helper and did everything for her; go to the store, get her medicine, whatever she needed. And in return, she was my solace and refuge from my loud family. She was my spiritual grandmother. We shared the same birthday—February 2nd, "Ground Hog Day." Now that I think of it, she probably knew the connection we had and that's why I was chosen by one of her prophets to befriend her in this life. There I was, a Catholic Italian girl learning some of life's lessons from the wisdom of her Jewish grandma.

I loved her much more than my own grandmother. I even risked the ruler in school from Sister. Sister had said that all Jews were horrible people and that they had killed Jesus Christ. My love for Mrs. Weiss told me that that couldn't be true and I said so. Sister sent me to the back of the room. Permanently. I didn't complain, though, because Mrs. Weiss never complained either, even though I knew some days arthritis would torture her as well as some of her memories. She never mentioned those things. She just sat there and made her dolls. And talked to me like no one else did. She never raised her voice and she never got angry. Not only did I think she was the kindest woman in my building, she was the kindest woman in all of Brooklyn.

Once, my friend Ronnie hit me over the head with one of the boy dolls she had made for us and blood gushed down my face. I knew it pained her to do so, but Mrs. Weiss threw the doll away. All of them. With her arthritic hands, she went through great pain to make these dolls and even though it broke her heart to get rid of them she still threw them away because it had caused someone else pain. I don't know if that was a good lesson or not, because I ache to have that doll now. But she surrendered to her ideals. I think that was the lesson she was trying to teach us. Not to live in the pain of the past but, rather, in the positive here and now. She could have gotten lost in the pain of her body, the pain of her memories, but she never did. She gave complete, unconditional love. I'm still trying to listen to her teachings, to overcome old hurts.

I love you, Nettie Weiss. I tell you this now because I didn't know how to say it then. When you weren't there anymore, your sister gave me a little statue of yours that I always liked. My mother thought I should have gotten more, because you liked me so much, but my mother was unkind. Only you and I know that what we shared for those few brief years cannot be represented by things. A statue, a doll. It's the memories I hold, the memories of you and your biscuits and your tea and the lessons. I listened and heard all that you had to say. I live with the memory of the dolls, even the one that cracked my head and made me bleed. But more than that, I live with the memory of you, of what you taught me, not the lessons of history, but the lesson of what it is to be a person, a human being, a Brooklyn woman of the world.

WHACK—I could feel my brain moving, settling after the blow. There she was, sitting on top of me. Wild. Naked. What a fucking *mignon*, a crazy Russian girl who's beguiled me here. I could have gone home much earlier. "Writing?!" she had said, "You have to get up in the morning to do writing? Why don't you stay up tonight and do some living?!" Seductive post-war logic, I took the bait. She looks like Mila Javovovich or whatever her name is. Well sort of a generic over the counter version. I'm lying on the hotel bed, on my back looking up at her. Not a very comfortable bed, I can feel metal underneath somewhere, sheets and blankets on the floor with our clothes. It is a pretty small room for the money I've paid, a polished wood and busy wallpaper job. There I was asking for grocery receipts from my daughter today and now I've thrown three times as much on this little extravaganza. Two small windows, open, face away from the Ocean towards Santa Monica. One window is up high, about six feet, giving the feeling that I am in a basement. *Notes From the Underground*. We had talked about Dostoevsky earlier at dinner, then tequila and cigarettes at La Cabana on Rose Ave. I think Trotsky got his ice pick in Mexico. I feel like I've been out of the country all night. And talking about Dostoevsky to a Russian is so frigging lame, I did it anyway. The TV is playing the History channel, and I shit you not, some special about the Red Army's march on Berlin in 1945. Artillery pieces are firing. Hitler is ranting. Stalin is staring. Soldiers are running over rubble. Churchill and Roosevelt nowhere to be found. I am still a little drunk, and my jaw was starting to sting. What the fuck did she do that for? Then it hit me. I should have been home tonight helping my daughter with her homework. I'll be rolling in around 5 A.M. sneaking into my room and pretending I came home at a decent hour. I deserved that slap I suppose. She channeled it from some grand scorecard, an assessment from the universe. Jesus, my head is going to hurt tomorrow. How in the hell did I get here? I am supposed to be looking for a girlfriend, some girl who looks good in her sandals and cashmere pashmina, soft wind swept and strolling along Abbott Kinney at golden hour. Instead, I am with a mystical, astrological, well-read, ill-fed, chain smoking Russian with the most incredible blue eyes. They glow. Neon half moons in the dark room. God, it shouldn't have to be like this. Then she laughs. A deep scary laugh from the depths of her 108 lbs. "I am sorry, Russian guys like that. I won't do it again."

It's the disguise
That keeps us safe
When fear threatens to stamp us invalid
It's also what traps us
Our very own house of reflection

The world plays on the cavern wall
We chase shadows as scripted
Plying our will only in the schism between the mind of chaos
And the microcosm of our individual program
All the while beyond the shadows lies the pure
If not for here, we wouldn't know there from anywhere

Struggle of a thousand lifetimes
Ask any mystic—Sufi, Sikh, Jew, Jain, Jehovah—and you'll hear the same
Still the stink, the kink, the rotting crotch of it is—
That all the holy rollin,' saffron robes, ahimsa—
Just gets woven into the fabric of the illusion
So much for being pure by acting pure

Incense rises with chant from the steppes of Chakragil
Reverend Andrew stomps and talks Katydid in the swamp
Kalil kneels and Hannah kneads
As if washing hubcaps and baking cobblestones into jackknives
Could stop the soul's perspiring

Oh would it be that the journey were so easy
Oh would it be that it were done at the time of our choosing
Oh would it be that it were done without us first making such a mess of things

But how else will I get comfortable with all the dark corners
Where need and pain
Lust and anger
Ego and avarice take hold
Maybe this is what will spur me
When I am fortunate enough to catch a glimpse of the pure
That I'll find the courage to navigate the schism
And peel the illusion to one side with both hands
By the layer
And see inside

71

Another day in pursuit of the authentic voice. Another day which started with an authentic migraine, complete with vomiting and distorted vision. And because it was too late to take my medication, I had to ride out the electric waves of pain until they faded away. I imagine this is like heroin withdrawal. Unfortunately, I had to drive to a conference while still under the effects of the migraine. But Eric gave me a plastic bag to set on the front seat, in case I threw up again while I was driving. So at seven o'clock in the morning I'm driving north on the 101, trying to cope with the sounds and smells and light that overwhelm you when you're on the tail end of a migraine. At the risk of not sounding authentic—it's like being in a blender with broken glass and a skunk's testicles.

Forty minutes later the headache was gone. I felt shaky and faint—and wondered if anyone at the conference could tell I had been sick earlier. But no one seemed to notice; in fact, no one really seems to see me at these things. I guess it's an elective invisibility. So I went outside during a break and sat on a bench. I heard a big squawk at my feet. I looked down and there was a nice brown duck blinking its beady eyes at me. The conference room is located at a hotel by a lake and I'd seen the ducks and swans and geese paddling around on the water earlier; I just hadn't seen any close up. "What a nice duck," I bent down to take a better look at his beady eyes. "Aren't you a pretty quacker."

He leaned against my leg. Squawk, quack, squawk. Message received. Feed me lady and no one gets hurt. I nodded and quietly made my way back into the conference room. I lifted a couple of bagels from the buffet table and then hurried back outside. The duck was still waiting for me, beady eyes gleaming. I tore a small piece of bagel and offered it to the duck, who I swear, was now smiling. Quack. Thanks lady. Big pieces, please. So I'm tearing pieces of bagel for this little beggar when I hear this screaming riot in back of us. I turn around and there is a horde of ducks and geese swimming towards me and this little brown duck and they look mad as hell. HONK, QUACK, SQUAWK, HONK, HONK. Now I'm surrounded by a vicious crowd of waterfowl and they're flapping their wings and nipping at my shoes and I only have one bagel left and I'm trying to quietly tell them, "Shoo, shoo," without anyone in the conference room seeing me surrounded by birds. But they're mad, they saw me feeding the little brown duck and they aren't going away. Then the worst thing happens—I'm holding the last sesame bagel when the biggest goose, and I mean this was a big goose, just pops up and takes the entire bagel out of my hand. The goose starts to waddle back to the lake with the bagel in his beak and all the other birds are after him, chasing him right back to the water. That's when I realize I'd better make a break for it, seeing as I am now bagel-less and surrounded by mad waterfowl. I start to edge back to the conference room door and I'm almost there when suddenly I turn around, and there's that damn little brown duck again. Quack. Hey lady, you going somewhere? I pretend I've never seen him before and walk into the conference room closing the glass door to make sure that I don't look back and get turned into a pillar of salt.

Hours later, an Important Speaker is giving the keynote speech in the conference and the all the suits in the room are hushed, listening with the mouths slightly open, breathing in shallow gasps, listening to the words and the silence in between them. Suddenly, there is a knock on the door. Someone gets up and goes to the side-paneled door and opens it and no one is there. A moment later the knock is heard again. The paneled door is opened again and no one is standing there. I turn and look out the glass door which overlooks the lake. Standing with his head cocked to one side is my little brown duck. He is pecking the glass door with his beak, waiting for that woman with the red hair to come back outside and give him that last lousy bagel she promised him. I laugh to myself. The headache from this morning seems very far away.

Mother always cried on December 17th.
It was the anniversary of the day she arrived
in America in 1938.
It was the day that marked
the final separation
between the old world and the new.
Every December 17th mother re-lived this day.
Born, Erna Bergen, my mother braved
the long ocean adventure alone
yet alongside hundreds of others
who were moving across the Atlantic Ocean
in December of 1938.
Each person carried excruciating baggage.
Mother never told me much
about her maiden voyage by ship,
but the sound of her maiden name
rang out clearly for more than
six decades in America.
Mother carried all the names with her.
She brought the Bergens, the Bodenheimers
and the Schiff families with her
from her homeland in Germany.
They spoke loudly through her skin and bones.
Her parents Max and Hedwig were wrapped
tightly around her heart and gut.
Her grandparents Malchen and Sannchen,
Max and Eve were alive in her brown eyes.
Aunt Sally, Aunt Rosa, Aunt Josephine,
Uncle Albert and the cousins
she grew up with came along inside her.
These relatives were invisible in my world,
yet fully alive in my mother's world.
Their ghosts floated around
New York and then across
the large continent of America
traveling with my mother
by Greyhound Bus to California in 1941.
My mother straddled two worlds . . .
the bold and courageous new life in America . . .
and the endless visions of political torture,
loss, separation, and annihilation

74

from her family and homeland
in Frankfurt, Germany.
While my mother's new life
was full of excitement and challenges,
her old life had become
hardened into her arteries
with layers of invisible scar tissue over her heart.
But every December 17th
everything became visible and clear.
Once a year my mother
lay all her bare bones and guts on the table.
It was her feast, her fast,
her purge, her binge,
her vomit, her consumption.
She displayed it all.
On that day I knew
that her life teetered
precariously between
privilege and deprivation.
She had been welcomed by a new homeland
yet cast out from her beloved Frankfurt.
She carried hope for over six decades,
working daily to avoid drowning
in her waters of despair.
By December 17th, 2002
mother was 89 years old.
She was empty of tears.
She had surrendered,
dry-eyed and peacefully.
My mother, Erna Bergen,
was beautiful even in death.
Her white hair continued to glisten even though her heart
and tears had stopped.
Her normally pink skin became rosy and warm.
I sat and watched peace
melt over her like a
warm, soft blanket.
She was still Erna Bergen.
She left quietly to join all
the other Bergens,
Bodenheimers and Schiffs.
Every December 17th tears
now make my green eyes sparkle . . .
like the green eyes of my grandmother I never knew.

A pearl ring on my left hand
reminds me of mother's arrival and departure.
Every December 17th
I see my mother's tears and face
in mine when I look in the mirror.
It's over yet we're not finished.
For better or for worse
even after death
there is something un-nameable
that continues into eternity.

76

I just got back from tea with Genieve, one of my dear lost long friends trapped in hair extensions, daily yoga and spinning wheels of stationary implants in rooms with no view. Genieve is engaged to a Rockefeller. She is getting married in March. . .no April. . .no, it's settled, May. Forty-plus, and no cryonic egg storage equals desperation.

The biggest fallout from the tech crash in the nineties for these women was the loss of their husband's money. Courtesans without a venue, they journeyed from Beverly Hill west to Santa Monica to mine Maha for men with balanced tree poses and flexible spines. They carried their child support in one hand and packing Harry Winston's on the other.

Genieve is happy today. She is sure he will not ask for a prenuptial. I want to say, 'He doesn't have to ask, you already gave it to him by accepting how he has treated you prenuptially—that's the agreement. You gave him your soul; he doesn't need a piece of paper.'

I am drifting in and out of the conversation. I can only concentrate on vapor so long without water. . .no alcohol. Even my Yerba alert has moved from red to amber after two cups.

Genieve is pleading her case with my jury sharing her process with God, her 10 year old daughter who has gained 25 pounds in one year, more than Genieve gained carrying her.

I keep cracking my toes inside my shoes and circling my ankles 1-2-3-4-5 to the right, 1-2-3-4-5 to the left, change foot.

We agreed on this spot because it is halfway between our two homes, not because we like it. We drove to Pasadena once for the best English tea in Southern California. But because we have become people who have succumbed to the belief that your day can be considered a success if you have not had to travel east of La Cienega—used to be La Brea—the best is measured in miles, not taste. Looking around I see how crowded it has gotten. It's a very popular place to be. How many restaurant owners would think halfway was a criterion for success?

A fat actress who wasn't able to parlay the condition into a television series stops by our table to say "hello." She is wrapped in a black and white tie dye nightmare from which I am sure she will never awaken. The second toe of her right foot, noosed in a ring, has long ago suffocated from too little reality. Her visit is interrupted by a call on her new "thin" cell phone which she introduced to us earlier. The mystery of accessories are revealed to me in this moment. If you can't be thin, accessorize thin. She wanders away from us and into conversation. I watch her cross the street to an area named by the city "Palisades Green," a patch of three-by-five grass that has three trees and two park benches. She lumbers around but never rests. A mother elephant looking for young she never had.

Genieve says, "Anyway, so he says, Do you see the love light coming out of my eyes?"

Before I can stop myself I say, "And how did you respond? Yes, and I hear the bullshit coming out of your mouth."

She looks at me and laughs. I think we have grown apart farther than I thought. Too sweet tea, too may hormone treatments, too much access in inner circles without inner core separate us.

Her eyes, rendered Anime from early age intervention, marshal together all their resources to express a tear.

"I love talking to you. Whenever I talk with you I feel heard."

"Hurt?" I said.

"No heard. I've been missing you."

I laugh with her and I think, 'No you've been missing yourself.'

Connor has never been to the Venice Canals before, but he likes what he sees along its weedy shoreline—the bohemian houses with their tiny docks and canoes. The quaint white footbridges that cross the water, connecting a maze of walkways. Connor brushes his blonde hair from his eyes and tells me, "If we had one of these homes, I could catch fish all day long." He holds a square plastic critter box that he grabbed from my Jeep, left there after our hike up Temescal Canyon. On that trip, he was hoping to catch a giant salamander in the waterfall. He surveys the still water of the canals and says, with a seriously helpful look on his face, "Mom, if we lived here we would never have to go to a pet store again." My son does not see the coke cans in the canal or the oily slicks that float on top of the water. No, he is determined to catch a fish or a crab. He has what I have—that desire to own a wild thing with the even wilder hope that it can live in captivity and that once possessed it can love us back the way we love it.

A Japanese family—with white caps on their heads and digital cameras around their necks—mutters past us. Next to us the dandelions sway, heavy with bees promiscuously spreading petals with their mutton legs. Suddenly, I want to tell Connor that I had a lover in one of those canal houses. He was a big-wave surfer with the insanely blue eyes of a tiger. He was in town after a winning a contest and on his way to wherever, and that was good enough for me—a girl who believed in love, at first sight. And that boy was mine, all mine, for a few stolen hours on a sweaty summer night, on dirty sheets, on a mattress on the floor, in the back room of someone else's canal house.

A duck lands in the middle of the water with wet flaps and snaps me back to the shit stained sidewalk and to Connor, who stands at the edge of the canal studying the glittering murk for fish. Quickly, he scoops his container through it and yells, "I got one!" A bit of silver with dark eyes swims chaotically and bashes into the plastic walls of the box. "Will my fish live?" Connor asks, cheeks flushed with the thrill. And even though I know how the story ends I tell him, "Probably not, but you can keep him."

How long could he live?" he asks me. He is so happy, I consider lying.

"Maybe a day." I say. His brow catches then releases.

"Hey, look at that!" Connor points at a flounder gliding next to the shore. "Can you capture him for me?" he begs.

"No, it's too big." I reply. We watch as the flounder searches for a place to hide. When it settles down, it will disappear.

"I want him!" Connor declares sadly, "I really want him." A cool wind chops the water until we cannot see the flounder, until we cannot separate it from the muck on the bottom of Abbot Kinney's dirty dream. We walk around ducks eating Mexican style rice off the sidewalks. On a deck, naked from the waist up, a surfer-type is drying his long hair. He smiles at me and I look down, afraid to want. A cloud blocks the sun then skitters away. The water in the critter box splashes crazily onto Connor's pants as he lifts it to his eyes. The sky has clouded over. The canal has turned dark. "It's time to turn around," I say, expecting protest, but he continues to study the frantic fish. When he lowers the box he says, "Mom, I want to let him go," his voice is firm. "I don't want to kill him." His blue eyes hold mine. Wild child. At twelve, so much more than I ever was.

Connor bends and gently dips the box back into the water and in a flash of hope the tiny bit of silver swims away.

I walk along the road
past fields of corn on one side
and soybeans on the other.
Next to an abandoned farm house
stands the remnants of a barn
with gaps between the naked boards
through which I can see cattle,
calm and still, inside.

I am this place, long grass,
flat prairie and distant hills,
ripening crops in August,
replaced by cold winds
and frozen earth in January,
always framed by river
and sandstone bluffs.
I am the sparrow
that catches bugs in flight,
weaves her nest
out of long, wild grass
and strands of hay.
I claim all this and a storm
of red-winged blackbirds
scared out by the harvester.

I wander here in the dark tunnel
made by full-grown corn,
so high, it hides the magic
from the magician
until I drink his potion
and grow tall enough
to see the sunflowers
at the borders of the field.

81

BOMBSHELTER PRESS

Anthologies

Twelve Los Angeles Poets (224 pp) $14.95

13 Los Angeles Poets (160 pp) $13.95

Moving Pictures: Nine Los Angeles Poets (62 pp) $5.00

Raising the Roof: Poets Supporting Habitat for Humanity, Riverside (72 pp) $10.00

The New Los Angeles Poets (203 pp) $12.50

Two-Women Show (Haft/Laumeister) (62 pp) $10.00

After I Fall (Alexander/Kulikov/Lee/Wilson) (64 pp) $8.95

Truth and Lies That Press for Life (216 pp) $12.95

4 Los Angeles Poets (ellen, Mima Pereira, Shirley Love, Anne Marple) (128 pp) $16.00

Books by Single Authors

Natural Selections (Elaine Mintzer) (120 pp) $16.00

A Lone Black Gull (Michael Andrews) (320 pp) $18.00

Coffin Lumber (Michael Andrews) (128 pp) $12.00

Breaking Down the Surface of the World (Jack Grapes) (62 pp) $10.00

Lucky Finds (Jack Grapes) (45 cards) $12.50

Chaos and Dancing Stars (Jean Katz) (140 pp) $15.95

Passion & Shadow (Judi Kaufman) (98 pp) $18.00

Crossing the Double Yellow Line (Stellasue Lee) (95 pp) $12.95

The Return of Sound (Zahava Sweet) (96 pp) $14.95

Corpses of Angels (Henry Morro) (72 pp) $12.95

ONTHEBUS

Double Issue 6/7 (330 pp.) $13.50
Charles Bukowski letters; interviews with David Mura & Joyce Carol Oates; provocative photo-essay by Penny Wolin, "The Jews of Wyoming."

Double Issue 8/9 (330 pp.) $13.50
Interviews with Allison Lurie, Anne Waldman, Thomas McGrath, Ai; color portfolio with poems by Pablo Picasso and surrealist paintings of his lover, Alicia Rahon.

Double Issue 10/11 (350 pp.) $13.50
Frida Kahlo full-color portrait & essay; last journals of Bukowski; interviews with Thylias Moss & Alice Notley; translations of Pablo Neruda.

Issue 12 (265 pp.) $11.00
Bukowski journals & photographs; interviews with Sharon Olds & Grace Paley; essay by Jack Grapes on the painting of F. Scott Hess.

Issue 13 (265 pp.) $11.00
Interviews with James Dickey & Tom Wolfe; Bukowski album of journals and poems.

Issue 14 (312 pp.) $11.00
Art by Susan Manders & Ruth Bavetta; Bukowski journals & poems; work by William Stafford, Ai, Donald Hall, Sam Hamill.

Double Issue 15/16 (324 pp) $15.00
Art by Ruth Bavetta & Susan Manders; Bukowski journals, letters, poems; interviews with Annie Dillard, Dorianne Laux, Kim Addonizio; drawings by Mindy Alper & Matt Wardell; work by Richard Jones, Lyn Lifshin, Ai, Suzanne Lummis, Katharine Harer, Kate Braverman, Charles H. Webb.

Double Issue 17/18 (332 pp) $15.00
Art by Susan Manders & James Doolin; Bukowski album; interviews with Arthur Miller, E. L. Doctorow, B. H. Fairchild; work by Katharine Harer, Lyn Lifshin, Suzanne Lummis, Doren Robbins, Bill Mohr, Kathleen de Azevedo, Henry Morro.

Double Issue 19/20 (288 pp) $15.00
Cover photo by Robert Durell; art by Aaron Smith; interview with John Irving; letters, journals, poems by Bukowski; translations of Yehuda Amichai, Gu Cheng,Táhirih, others; 20 reviews; writing by Steve Kowit, Richard Jones, Harry Northup, Michael C. Ford, Bill Mohr.

www.bombshelterpress.com
BOMBSHELTER PRESS
PO Box 481266 Bicentennial Station
Los Angeles CA 90048 USA